The
ALL
KNOWING
Diary

The Truths You Were Never Told
How To Harness ALL KNOWING
To Make The Right Decisions Every Time

Daniel Rechnitzer

To Joe and Sara, without you, your
inspiration, your love, your patience and
truth, none of this would have been
possible. Eternally you, Daniel.

The ALL KNOWING Diary
The Truths You Were Never Told

By Daniel Rechnitzer

© Copyright 2011, Daniel Rechnitzer

Publisher: Ui Ink Pty Ltd

Illustrator: Sonja Rechnitzer

USA publication prepared by Maria 'Molly' Morelli

ISBN 978-0-9807827-1-4

1st edition, 2011

Paper used in the production of this book is from pulp sourced from sustainable forest plantations.

'ALL KNOWING'

Omniscience [om·nis·cience] / Sanskrit: सर्वज्ञ

1. The quality or state of being omniscient.
2. Infinite knowledge.
3. Make the right decisions every time.

SKEPTICISM

We see only what we believe. The less we allow ourselves to believe, the less we see and therefore the less we experience. So much of our life is a result of what we believe that it becomes almost impossible to distinguish truth from belief. Read this book with an open mind, so as to allow in a greater reality—one where everything becomes possible. Where life can expand instead of contract, where you become the driver of an expansive Universe that responds exactly to your thoughts.

"When you allow in more, you see more, you become more; and so you experience more!"

Contents

Glossary

All Knowing

A capability we, as human beings, have access to through Whole Brain Intelligence.

Clearing

Seeing what is real; to remove the past from your current experience of life.

Ego

The opposite of Truth. A version of your SELF that traps the mind into perceiving your beliefs over your True Self, thereby creating an illusion, a false reality—the opposite to what brings happiness.

Language Of The Body

Intuitive messages and/or physical symptoms stemming from the body, to bring what's currently Subconscious (and/or True Self) into conscious awareness.

Root Cause Of Illness

The 'thoughts,' 'beliefs,' or 'emotions' generating symptoms in the body.

Soul Purpose, Life Purpose

A series of decisions that lead to fulfilment, growth, and contribution to you and your world, coming from within—your Soul and your intuition.

Spirituality

The creators of what we call 'physical reality'—layer
upon layer of intelligent energy, 'thought' in other words,
holding an intention to give a specific experience to
those within physical reality.

Super Conscious Mind, Soul, Higher Self, True Self

These words are used interchangeably. They are one
and the same. It is an All Knowing, pure energy, pure
intelligence. It is that part of you that gives life, that is
pure Consciousness, pure nature. It is YOU—the one you
can trust for guidance.

Thought

The non-physical Universe.

Ui, Universal Intelligence

A field of intelligence all life in the Universe draws
on, the sum total of energy in the Universe. It is pure
intelligence, All Knowing.

Whole Brain Intelligence

The two halves of your brain connecting as one,
optimizing brain function and bringing you information
beyond your own stand-alone knowledge. We call it the
'Antenna Brain'—the human internet.

Introduction

My life has been a transition from feeling I need to be more, to recognizing and understanding who and what I really am. This is life for many of us. We all begin life searching for answers: Who am I? Am I wanted? Where do I belong? Am I loved? We start off with so many questions and although the answers are available, many of us are left to discover the truth by ourselves.

Life could be so much simpler if we were all told the truth right from the start. So much time is wasted while the youth fight for an identity, later to become adults who would do almost anything to keep this identity, at great cost to themselves and the world around them. Life is an unveiling of what is real. Over time, lessons are learned, truth is restored, and happiness is gained.

But what if this could all happen right from the beginning? What if struggle and not knowing the answers became a thing of the past? Is it possible?

So, where do we go? Who has all the answers?

We all do!

So much of society is built upon the premise that we are without answers, that life has to be a fight, that we have forgotten some fundamental truths about being human. Who are we to think that we are extraordinary?

We have all developed our own opinions about life, love, and the Universe, yet so many of our opinions are no longer working for us. We are creating less balance, more struggle, and less happiness than our ancestors.

The good news is that this era of not knowing who we really are is coming to an end. The absence of knowing is being bridged by a truth that lies deep within every single one of us. The truth is we all carry the answers within, like a blueprint for our existence.

You see, our truth exists within every molecule of our bodies. It surrounds us and cocoons us with life-giving light, without which life would cease to exist.

So many on Earth view life as a fluke, as random acts of molecules colliding. But in fact, something far more profound has occurred. Life is purposeful, life is nature, and nature equals harmony and precision. We too exist within these parameters. We too are perfect in every way. The perfection that we witness in nature lies equally within ourselves. There are no accidents here. The human form is one of the Universe's proudest creations. We can sing, dance, mimic the creative forces of nature to create life—all through intention. Could there be anything more sublime?

Often, the most obvious answers are staring us right in the face. In the case of the sublime being mirrored right back to us, this could not be more true.

Like in a still pond, what is above is mirrored below— the sublime that surrounds us is the sublime contained within.

It's time to realize your greatness and your importance.

This Diary attempts to capture the very essence of what is currently missing from humanity, to aid a reconnection with our very nature—All Knowing.

On this journey, you will read about our true nature, our belief systems, how these affect our reality and how our truth lies hidden underneath. You will explore how your reality may be holding you back, and how the Ego, a parallel Universe, tricks us into believing what is not the truth. You will discover immense capabilities, new realities waiting for you and some ancient tools to take you there. Together with your inner wisdom, you can unleash your true nature—ALL KNOWING.

You will see clues everywhere—in words, poems, pictures and exercises. Piece these together and the journey into the sublime unknown will begin ...

My Questions

How did this life happen, this body, this Earth?
So many questions, answers I feel I deserve!
Why do I struggle, why am I here?
So many questions, answers I can't bear!
What is it that is still missing?
Isn't there more than simply wishing?
Am I not everything I can be?
I have followed others' advice endlessly.
I am someone with needs and ambition,
But where are the answers to fulfil my mission?
What is this source of Nature, of life?
Clearly, it's intelligence with great might!
Am I part of this intelligence, is it mine to shine?
What is it about my brain, how do I align?
What is the truth to all my dilemmas?
If I seek answers, will life really get better?

Questions I Have...

Have You Ever Wondered ...

How we got here? How we came to be?

I have!

Have you ever wondered who or what intended the body the way it is? How our mind works—our awareness, our ideas and our very instincts? Who or what programmed us? Who put man and woman together with an explosive orgasm? How does a child come to be? Why do planets orbit around the sun?

How was life conceived? Who designed birds, the stripes on a zebra, or a tiger's camouflage? Is language really the extent of how we can communicate? How do we pick up on another person's presence—their anger or excitement? How do so many see, hear, or feel a person's 'spirit' (their Soul, their True Self), yet so many others still go on ignoring this reality?

Why do so many people "know better," but are still stuck doing what brings them harm or unhappiness? Why do so many people not want to change a thing about life, but still complain about how unfulfilled they are? Why do so many people drink, smoke, and have affairs, yet give advice on how to run a company, or even a country, when they clearly do not even have their own life in order?

Why do sports stars, models, and movie stars make riches, while enlightened healers are expected to work for free?

I have wondered about all this and so much more.

I believe our imagination holds the key. It's in our imagination that answers come.

But isn't our imagination just all made up?

Or is it?

Who is to say that what is "made up" is any less real than the reality we live by? What if our imagination was more than we know? What if we have it all backwards? What if there is no fixed reality at all, other than the one we believe in? Like a dream that feels so real ...

What is real?

Don't our dreams feel real? If it is all just a dream, what if we could all control it? Who is the dreamer?

What would you dream?

What are the rules in this dream? Is ANYTHING possible in this dream?

Let's find out ...

What Is This Diary, Really?

This is an expedition—not to the center of the earth, but to the center of me ...

This Diary explains what happened. It chronicles my insights on my journey within. It is also an invitation for you to connect with something truly infinite and magnificent.

I had always wondered what is at the core of my being? Do the answers really lie within? What will I find there? And most importantly, how would I even get there?

How does one steer a ship that doesn't exist? What is my heading?

This Diary details my journey inward and the answers I received when asking the questions that had plagued me for many years. This is my truth, my adventure— hopefully it will open the door for you to discover yours.

It Begins ...

My Head Spins With Questions And It Is Time For Answers!

What if our world is us, mirrors us, and reflects us in every way? Are we destroying it as we destroy ourselves?

What if each human being represents how 'God' works—each human being having a conscious awareness of itself, an ability to power our thoughts, an uncanny ability to experience itself in accordance with the thoughts it creates?

What if life gives us clues to the real picture, but we continuously ignore them to suit our needs? Are we being told something in our everyday? Who is listening? Clearly, not many of us.

What if our sun represents something greater, an insight into the greater working of ourselves, life, and what is at the heart of the Universe? A ball of light powering it all—our source of life?

What if mankind is lost right now, struggling to find its way, sheep without their shepherd? Where has our shepherd gone?

What if our intelligence is not a factor of DNA or our genes, but rather of our ability to see ourselves in a particular way?

What if our nature wasn't self-destructive, but something else—self-loving? What would life look like then and how do we access this self-loving nature? What if religion and science were on the same side? Surely that would help society resolve many issues. What if I could access all answers to any one of my questions at the speed of thought? What if I had ALL the answers? How would my life change?

What if we all had access to all the answers? How would we evolve as a species?

So many unanswered questions ...

Why, Why, Why?

Why do I wake in the middle of the night, hovering six feet above my body, looking down, feeling weightlessness like a light puff of smoke, but aware of myself? How is this possible?

How do I know things before they happen? I see them in my mind's eye, sometimes months before. Why?

I can feel a person's thoughts, their moods, and their pondering mind. Why?

I walk into a room and I can feel the anger that has been present. How is this possible?

I receive a phone call from a friend moments after I thought of them. Coincidence or purpose? A flash of genius strikes when I least expect it, profoundly simple solutions to agonizing life challenges. Where did this insight come from?

We all experience amazing coincidences, synchronicities, signs, and omens. Where do they come from? Who is the architect of fate and destiny? Are they all just coincidences? I know this is not the case.

My body responds to my thoughts; I lift a finger by a thought; I react to sexual thoughts ... What reactions does my body have to negative, self-hating thoughts? Does it die because of these thoughts? Is it immune to these thoughts, but responsive only to positive thoughts? Not a chance. What does this mean? What have we missed?

A child and its mother, somehow in sync—does it stop there? Are we all in sync? Why, and for what purpose? I can feel people's thoughts, solutions to people's health flood into my mind, as if their emotions talk to me. Their hearts tell me why they have an illness. I know what's at the cause! It can be difficult to hear, but I know the answer.

An intelligence seems to be present in the design and functioning of the human form, so brilliant this design— eyes, ears, mouth, run, walk, eat, jump, think, create ... Sounds sublime, doesn't it? What is the source of this intelligence? If it is part of us, can we access it too?

Nature, ecosystems to perfection, a miracle everywhere the eye can see. Yet, so many people question its origins. Again, is this intelligence directly related to our origins? Can we harness it for our individual lives? Is it our nature? Have we lost touch with our nature?

It must be accessible! But how? Our beliefs change so often, scientific beliefs disproven one after the other. Why then do so many people cling to them like they are fact? Is enlightenment the absence of a belief system, allowing us to see what is really true? Beliefs are like anchors—should we be attached to them? How are they harming us?

My mind holds answers, they come to me as ideas. What else does my mind know that I don't? Are the answers all within? What is a mind, anyway? Is it my brain or just something my brain learns to access? Or is it more? Intuition strikes! What is intuition? Is it real? I feel a full body sensation, telling me the right decision to make. It pays off! Why? What is the source of this inspiration, this so-called 'intuition'? Is it my thoughts? Is my intuition more than that? Is it actually

All Knowing? How can it be?

So many questions, with so few answers right now!

More Questions ...

What is the truth? Who holds the answer? Science? Religion? Neither? What is enlightenment? Why do so few seek it? What does it promise that people fear? Is enlightenment the key to mastery over life?

I must take a stand. When the world is so topsy-turvy, one could look at the 'norm' and do the exact opposite. The norm: the bulk of Earth's population, seemingly consumed by wanting more, having more, or being seen as more. Is it not just about 'being' more? What holds us back from allowing simplicity—the simple truth—back into our lives? Why must we all climb mountains, build monuments, cross rivers just to be happy? Was this the intention, the overall plan, to consume nature's resources to make life worth living? Once again, in this topsy-turvy world, I'll be betting on the opposite.

Someone once told me the Bible was the best-selling book of all time ... and yet so many are still confused, still unhappy, miserable to the core, and getting worse!

So what's still missing from the Bible? What's still missing from life?

Now What?

Who do I turn to when so much eludes me?

I am without answers, without understanding of life.

I have reached the point of misery. Does someone else know, or are the answers really inside. How do I get to them? How can I know?

Something has to change ... I have to change!

But how?

Where to Turn?

I Remember A Voice

Inside Me

Years ago, I knew it was me,
It used to have me feel so free,
It used to have me feel complete,
When now all I feel is incomplete.
What is missing that I should know,
That will bring me back into the flow?
I used to know how to be glad,
I used to know what made me sad.
Now I need to know what's true,
What in my life has left me blue?
Stuck in a hole, with oh, no light,
I've clearly failed to do what's right.
Help me to see just what is real ...
I need to know, so I can heal.
I began asking questions, I knew someone could hear,
I knew in my bones I had nothing to fear.
How could I have gone wrong all these years?
I knew that the answers just had to be near.
I knew through and through, there was more to me,
There was so much more for us all to see.
I once knew a truth inside of me.
My life stood still, but I always knew,
I was destined for more than this Ego stew.
Like a voice that knew just what was true,
Was it part of me, or something I knew?

14

How do I connect to my wisdom, to my truth?
How do I survive, paving the way, as living proof?
I sat down to hear this voice,
I stilled my mind to have no noise.
Then it happened ...
Like a flash of insight telling me so,
I had followed the footsteps of a foe.
A message came through, a sense and a feeling,
I had lost my way because of my yearning.
What I believed had done me wrong,
Now I was stuck in a life that hit like a bomb.
To follow my nose, that was the key,
To listen and act on what's inside of me.
To let go of what others told me was "right,"
To follow instead my inner light.
What could this mean?
I knew of no light.
The voice inside chuckled, grew loud and clear,
Everything true that rang in my ear:
"Follow my way and you'll plainly see,
Infinite possibility inside of me.
I'm your teacher now, I am YOU,
Listen good and you'll live anew.
To question my guidance will end in tears ...
You're not the one who's been around all these years.
I'll guide you clearly, that's a fact.
With me within you, there's no holding back.
I'm more than you know; it's hard to show,
I'm the secret within ... I am, that is so!
Hold your pen and hold it tight,
Listen to me and you'll be bright.

You'll see a new world, from old to new,
One busting to come from inside of you.
Listen to me and listen good,
Follow my footsteps, you'll be understood.
There's truth in my words, you'll clearly see,
To listen to others, you'll fail dismally.
I'm one with you, we're one together,
Sober up and we'll live forever.
Talk to me each day and night,
You and I both can shine our light.
Today begins a journey of exploration,
One that will go beyond your expiration.
This work that you do,
Bring truth to the world—that is you!
The world is awakening to a new ideal,
That what's within is what is real.
Persist through the tough times, they'll get lighter,
We're on a journey that's faster and brighter.
Follow my voice every step, to the letter,
And everything you experience will get much better.
I'm not a voice outside your head,
I'm not lying in your neighbor's bed.
Instead, I'm invincible—that is true,
I'm the Universe living inside of YOU!
But there's something more that you should know,
There's more to you than you could know ...
Allow me in and I'll explain,
There's something special within your brain.
Take the two halves and make them whole,
Unravel the mysteries and truth will be told.
The voice you hear:Am I fiction, in your thoughts?

Or is there something more for all to be taught?
I am Body, Mind, and Soul,
It's what makes us all whole!
But wait, sit still and listen to me,
I have five Truths that will end the mystery.
These Truths are precious, like sacred stones,
I give them to you, but not to own!
It's time I hand you the keys
To help you all unlock ... INFINITY!"
And the messages kept coming through ...

Truth 1

You Are Not Who You Think You Are

"Reality Is Not What You See, But Rather What You Believe."

Who Am I?

Who you believe yourself to be is not the truth.
A version of you is all you see, not the real you
that you aspire to be. Rid yourself of this fiction,
there's more to you than this affliction.

Beliefs = Your Reality

The beliefs you hold dictate your reality. So much of what you see, hear, feel or say is a direct result of the beliefs you hold. Your health, your life success, your relationships and your children all reflect what you believe to be true. In fact, everything you experience reflects the beliefs you hold about life.

In an existence made of 'thought,' that which one believes is that which one experiences.

Beliefs are the views you have about yourself and your world. They are formed continuously, starting at a very young age and—unless corrected—continue to dictate your experiences of life. Your reality is indistinguishable from your beliefs.

You hold your beliefs consciously and Subconsciously.

Your conscious beliefs are the ones you know about— they are what drives your conscious decision making … to an extent. As the Subconscious Mind holds far more beliefs than your Conscious Mind, it plays a far bigger part in how you experience your reality.

Everything you believe about yourself, this life and the reality you belong to—good and bad—is stored in your Subconscious Mind. It is your Subconscious beliefs that are actually running the show, like a program running underneath your awareness.

These Subconscious beliefs are the programs that run your conscious beliefs and decisions. So, as much as you may try to concentrate consciously on specific objectives, affirmations, or beliefs, if this is not supported at the Subconscious level—or 'programming'—then this conscious effort may not ever create the changes you desire.

As children, we quickly make sense of our lives by forming beliefs. Our experiences—good and bad— have us decide things about ourselves and our world. Sometimes we form empowering beliefs such as "I am a genius." Other times (usually more often than not), we form disempowering beliefs such as "I'm not enough." Many beliefs are handed down to you, if you like, through parents, teachers and the media. Some classics include:

∞ "Money does not grow on trees."

∞ "No pain, no gain."

∞ "It is human nature to hurt ourselves."

∞ "Life was not meant to be easy."

∞ "This is a dog-eat-dog world."

Strip away past experiences from your body

Observing your parents as you grow up is a big source of input to your belief systems. Your father coming home from work and each day being asked by your mother: "How was work?", to which he responds "Stressful!", shapes your beliefs about working. So, you as a child already take on the belief that work is "stressful" and you embody that wherever you are engaged in "work," be it school, a project and, later in life, your profession.

You may have heard your parents repeat: "You can't trust the rich," or use the term "the filthy rich" when they talk. Well, knowing that all beliefs lead to experiences, guess how that belief affects you? Subconsciously, you don't want to be seen as untrustworthy, so you don't ever allow yourself to become rich. Beliefs are the beginning of all self-sabotage, and you don't even know you are doing it—it is Subconscious.

As a child growing up, beliefs are formed so easily.

Take, for example, a child who shows Mom and Dad their drawing, but Mom and Dad are busy at the time and tell that child to "Get out of the kitchen." Unbeknown to the child, Mom and Dad simply didn't want to accidentally spill the hot dinner on them and consequently hurt their loved child. However, without that information, the child feels rejected and begins to believe he or she is unimportant, or not creative. The child spends the rest of its life living through this reality, as if that belief was the truth. As an adult, career choices are influenced by this belief; relationships, financial

---

Your thoughts can harm other people,
be careful what you think of others

situations, health, destructive behaviors like drug or alcohol abuse—it dictates that person's entire future trajectory, with this person forever compensating in life to combat this inner belief and feeling within.

We all have so many beliefs that were created just like that—innocently—but we are living our lives as though these extrapolations were true.

Your beliefs about what is or is not possible are the sole determinant of how you experience your reality.

Some beliefs empower you to an extent, but it is important to understand the role of beliefs, as many of them have ceased working for you and have begun to work against you. As so many of your beliefs are inaccurate, they need to be changed to let in a more fulfilling life experience.

Who you believe yourself to be right now is not who you really are—just a limited version of what's real. Remove those beliefs that tell a lie and you'll learn to fly!

The lack of empowering beliefs about what it means to be a human being is the reason many on Earth struggle.

Ultimately, beliefs are responsible for how you are using your brain in the least efficient manner, but more on that later.

Beliefs actually dictate your behaviors, like a thermostat on a heater. They either switch you on to creating success, or switch you off and into sabotaging success. If you reach the full extent of whom you believe yourself to be and what your reality consists of, you feel a sense of unease in your body, often cutting you off from expanding yourself and moving forward. Instead, you do what you always do and revert back to self-sabotage. Those who are aware of this pattern are better equipped to push on, past the fears and sense of panic, and then move on to greater experiences of life.

So your beliefs can often create a new path, an alternate path from the one you were originally intending for yourself. Until a belief is recognized as just that—a belief—it is ultimately the 'master' of your destiny, choosing the pathway of your life.

On an even larger scale, your beliefs form an identity for yourself—one insecure and unsure of itself, an alternate identity to what is actually truth. Your beliefs hide the real version of you, the true version of your reality and what it actually consists of—just like a massive brick wall standing in your path.

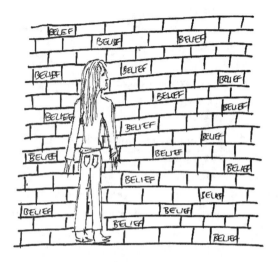

You do not see reality as it could be,
you see reality as you are.

Removing and scrutinizing your belief system is a
necessity if you are to change your ways. Many people
live their whole life thinking a belief is correct, only
to sadly find out after many missed opportunities that
it was simply a belief, not truth. This is why so many
people repeat patterns over and over again. This process
is simply our belief system trying to reveal itself to the
Conscious Mind for healing out your life experience.

Beliefs govern all. Your limiting beliefs are those that do
you the most harm.

Cultivate silence and stillness

Creating your reality through goal setting, positive affirmations, visualizations and focused intent is still subject to your beliefs.

> *One cannot conceive what*
> *one does not truly believe.*

If your beliefs are not in alignment with your goals, they will be met with hefty self-sabotage. You may want something on a conscious level, such as to be wealthy, but this does not correlate with the beliefs held in the Subconscious Mind that you are, for example, "not worthy" or "I don't want to be rich because rich people can't be trusted." The Subconscious belief is infinitely stronger than your conscious desire for something, so this is where you need to start if you want to create a new reality.

> *If you don't believe, you won't receive!*

Your beliefs need readjusting to support your goals ... worthwhile goals. More importantly, your beliefs need reviewing, as many of your current goals stem from your belief systems, often leading you toward goals that leave you feeling empty instead of fulfilled.

> *Your reality—what you perceive to be real—*
> *is a figment of your imagination. You imagine*
> *something to be true, so it is. You imagine*
> *yourself to be wrong, so you will be.*

Our entire reality is governed by beliefs—intersecting beliefs. You experience on an individual level what your individual beliefs are. In addition, you experience at a family level what beliefs you hold as a family; you experience as a community or nation what beliefs we hold as a community or nation, and so on. To transform these individual and collective experiences, you as an individual must change your own beliefs first.

Your reality is just a projection of your beliefs, of all our beliefs.

***Your reality is not what is true,
it is simply the world inside of you.***

It is a commonly held belief that people do not change—and so they don't. How can people change when the bulk of their beliefs stay the same throughout life? The reason their beliefs stay the same is because they do not yet have the tools to remove these unsupportive beliefs at the Subconscious level. So, it is simple. Let us stop condemning people for never changing and start teaching them how to shift their beliefs to supportive, creative ones.

The good news, as you may have realized by now, is that our beliefs are not real—they are a version of the truth, one that has been misinterpreted, often from a young age. Many originated from a state of mind that was disconnected with reality, unsure of itself. We made up our beliefs in this state, one that confused what it was feeling with what is truth. This happened repeatedly as we were young and continues as a pattern in our adult years.

Our beliefs started out based on something that was untrue or misinterpreted. If we make decisions based on something that was untrue to begin with, we then create experiences that are untrue for us now! And so it makes sense that so many of us are miserable and find happiness and fulfilment so elusive. So many people are living a life based on beliefs that were never true to begin with. Is it then any wonder that the world is in such disarray right now?

How Many Beliefs Are True?

Count the number of times you, or someone you know, have at one time believed something to be real, only later to discover the fallacy of it all. People bet their entire way of life on such beliefs. Some classic limiting beliefs we as human beings have believed so deeply in, and therefore made decisions because of, include:

∞ The earth is flat

∞ Men are superior to women

∞ Black people are inferior to white people

∞ Smoking is not bad for you

∞ Everything that can be invented has already been invented

∞ With war comes peace

∞ A business exists to make money, no matter the cost or damage it causes

∞ It's fine to pollute your planet, that's just the cost of progress

∞ Animals are inferior to human beings

It is lucky for all of us that these beliefs did not go unchecked … or did they?

How many of your beliefs are untrue? It is time to find out, because they're ruling the roost!

You see, it is impossible to find true happiness when we let our false beliefs create our life. The more beliefs we have, the harder it is to discover happiness. Beliefs want to be validated and so they create the very experience they are based on. Because they are based on something unreal, they are leading us away from what is real and away from that which actually brings happiness.

> *Fulfilment comes from making decisions based on what is true and real, not what is false and made up.*

But understand this: your beliefs are not set in stone, they are just frequencies of energy or thought that have not yet left your body. You hold on to them, because at a particular time you decided that these thoughts are actually who you are and therefore belong to you. You identified with them and, short of having the truth to identify with, you clung to these beliefs as a reference point for yourself and your reality.

Appreciate nature's abundance

The good news is that beliefs are not intrinsically who you are, rather they are just a shadow reflection.

The greater the stillness within your thoughts, the easier the Subconscious Mind can be 'reprogrammed,' throwing out the old beliefs and making room for something more productive, with greater possibility— infinite possibility. It is in your Subconscious Mind that your beliefs are organized and limiting beliefs can be removed with ease.

At the heart of all experiences are the thoughts and beliefs you hold about them. The physical reality simply reflects the beliefs held about it.

Be mindful, many people fall into the trap of holding on to beliefs to justify the decisions they have made to date, to avoid invalidating their life choices so far. This is a stubbornness you cannot afford—not if achieving fulfilment is important to you and for the very reason that our beliefs also dictate our health.

Learning to look at yourself through fresh eyes is enlightening! It is actually the definition of enlightenment—a mind unconstrained by its belief system.

The Less You Believe, The Less You Conceive

The less new supportive beliefs you let in, the harder it is to experience happiness. This is why the "know-it-alls" are the least happy people—they are stuck in a reality that cannot let in new perspectives and therefore new experiences. Skeptics suffer the most because the less open we are to the new, the less of life we can let in.

A closed mind is a luxury we as a species can no longer afford! It is time we accepted that underneath all the self-doubt there is an extraordinary being, sublime in every way. The only thing in the way of accessing this is the doubt that it exists.

It is important to find out what beliefs are holding you back, as altering these will literally provide you with a totally new experience of being alive. Reality shifts in direct proportion to the beliefs you let go of.

To shift a disempowering experience in life requires simply to shift the beliefs creating that very experience. Reality reflects the belief. Change the belief and your reality realigns.

Contemplate just how different your life would look if you had a totally different set of beliefs—beliefs that support your life's desires. The trick is to realize that even now—as you are reading this—your beliefs are

31

either pushing you toward success, or holding you back from discovering the truth that your beliefs were simply that—just beliefs! The good news is, if you are able to let that in, you have already taken the first step toward reshaping your life in a positive way!

Are you facing toward learning how best to remove your limiting beliefs, or away from it? Are you facing toward your True Self, or away? Are your beliefs supporting your successful endeavors, or are your beliefs sabotaging your success at each and every opportunity?

Be mindful, your beliefs feel real—they are designed to.

Do Beliefs Affect Our Body?

Your body is a mirror reflection of your belief system. It is your most direct feedback loop of what you believe your reality consists of. This is because your beliefs are held not just in your head (Subconscious Mind), but, importantly, also within your body. They are stored within the part of the body that governs the area in which your particular beliefs are held.

For example, beliefs that relate to fears of childbirth are aptly stored within the reproductive system. Beliefs you hold regarding your ability to stand up for yourself and be the man/woman you hoped to be are also stored within the same region—as are beliefs about your creative ability. Similarly, beliefs about responsibility and the need to carry other people's burdens are carried—

guess where?—the shoulders and neck ... and so on and so forth.

For years we have heard the phrases: "He carries the weight of the world on his back" (sore back), "Stop shouldering all that responsibility" (tight shoulders), "I was livid" (liver issues), "I can't look at another X" (eye problems)...These sayings are a dead giveaway to where we store thoughts and beliefs. It is how our body keeps our Conscious Mind abreast of the content within our Subconscious, a form of healing if you like.

Your illness, your pain, or a symptom in your body is your body attempting to restore balance to its ecology and natural equilibrium that has been disturbed by your untrue beliefs. The closer your beliefs are to the truth, the healthier your life and body.

Truth heals the body; non-truths age the body (yes, take that as an anti-aging hint!).

All beliefs carry a frequency. Some restore health and well-being, while others destroy it. Guess which beliefs do that?

Beliefs Are The Key

At every level, your beliefs are governing what you can or cannot access for yourself as part of this 'reality' we call life: the body, your experience of life, a fast

---

Remove all limiting beliefs

metabolism, finding a perfect partner, accessing pure genius, peace within—all 'experiences' are being governed by our belief systems. There is more to you than you know!

You are not your beliefs, but so much more. The less limiting beliefs you carry, the more of your true nature is allowed in—your True Self! Create stillness and the whole truth of who you are will make its way into your being.

In the end you will discover there is actually only one Universal belief worth holding. We shall discover what this is on our journey together. After all, it is currently why you are here ... to discover what is real.

Beliefs, Not Me!

I am not my beliefs, they are not me—
Beliefs create my reality, but don't set me free.
Beliefs are not real, they are imagined,
A version of the truth I once imagined.
Create a new reality, one that works,
A new experience of life, one that doesn't hurt!
Change your beliefs and you'll be glad,
That in truth not one of us is bad.
Enter your mind, it's time to reset.
A new life awaits, it's time to collect!

Are We Self-Destructive?

For years, people have been led to believe that it is in our nature to do harmful things. Is it in our nature to destroy ecosystem after ecosystem? Is it really human nature to cause harm to ourselves and others?

No, this is simply a belief. As we are born of nature and it is not within nature to do these things, it is not within our nature to do these things either.

Where these acts come from is quite the opposite—it is by being disconnected from our nature that has us resort to violence and self-destructive behaviors.

Disconnection from our nature has created a void, a void that we will do anything to fill. Reconnect back to your nature—all nature—and peace can be restored.

What Are The Main Limiting Beliefs Holding Humanity Back Right Now?

The following are a collection of the current most damaging beliefs held by human beings right now. Let us myth-bust these beliefs and learn the truth, so we can be set free to create greater possibilities in our lives.

∞ **Belief:** I am just a human being
  Truth: I am the Universe packaged into a walking, talking creation machine

∞ **Belief:** Everything we knew thousands of years ago was right and still applies today
Truth: Today we carry different beliefs and, consequently, our reality is different. We have developed the ability to accept more about our nature, so it's time to stop restricting our present reality based on what we could accept in the past.

∞ **Belief:** Love is a luxury, not a necessity for me and others
Truth: Without love our bodies deteriorate

∞ **Belief:** Science is at the forefront of discovery
Truth: Scientists are not enlightened, so their information is intrinsically limited

∞ **Belief:** I must do the right thing by my family
Truth: I must do the right thing by me and my well-being

∞ **Belief:** I'm running out of time to be successful, I have to get there fast
Truth: Perfect timing exists for me when I am All Knowing and accessing my true nature

∞ **Belief:** Science and spirituality are different
Truth: Science is and was created by 'spirituality,' as thought preceded creation

∞ **Belief:** Things happen to me, not because of me
Truth: I—we all—play the key role in my reality. I only need to change my beliefs to change my experiences

∞ **Belief:** Enlightened leaders care more about trees than the economy

Truth: Enlightenment is about balance. The traditional government places excessive focus on politics and the economy, creating an imbalance

∞ **Belief:** If I don't know it, it doesn't exist
Truth: The Universe is full of concepts I, as a human being, can't possibly fathom while I see myself with such limited eyes

∞ **Belief:** 'God' is outside of me, rather than within me
Truth: My beliefs block the truth—Consciousness is all there is, it is my intrinsic nature

∞ **Belief:** The economy is what makes the world tick
Truth: The economy is simply an indication as to how we value ourselves. Love makes the world tick

∞ **Belief:** I die at sixty to eighty years of age
Truth: I, as a human being, can easily live way beyond these years in current times, it's just our belief systems that age the body prematurely

∞ **Belief:** Illness is a frailty of the human body, not related to human thought
Truth: Illness is human thought being frail

∞ **Belief:** Parenting is for everyone, irrespective of their training
Truth: All parents can be great, but not all parents' beliefs lead to great parenting

∞ **Belief:** Politics has to be a game
Truth: Games don't create fulfilment; enlightened leaders do

Be present at all times

∞ **Belief:** Money is the only real measure of success
Truth: Happiness is the most accurate measure
of success

∞ **Belief:** Imagination is fiction, not reality
Truth: It is imagination as pure Consciousness
that is the true reality

∞ **Belief:** Anyone I am attracted to can be my perfect
match
Truth: Not everyone is of comparable soul evolution
to myself (i.e. my Soul Mate)

∞ **Belief:** Learning can only happen in the physical
world
Truth: Visit the Universe university—everything is
thought, thought is everywhere! Start downloading
now!

∞ **Belief:** We are the only ones in the Universe
Truth: Life permeates the entire Universe, that's the
point

∞ **Belief:** When I die, that's it, there's nothing else
Truth: When I die, I will simply wake up

∞ **Belief:** We are all disconnected from one another
Truth: All life is Consciousness—connected and All
Knowing

∞ **Belief:** Entertainment must come externally
Truth: Your True Self is very entertaining when you
start listening

∞ **Belief:** Failure is a prerequisite to success
Truth: Failure comes from drawing on your belief
system instead of All Knowing.

Have My Beliefs Taken On A Life Of Their Own? Am I Real?

To truly know myself I must have an opposite, but following my opposite will not bring happiness.

Over time a Consciousness builds, using all your beliefs as its identity. The more beliefs you carry, the stronger is the identity that is created. This form of Consciousness seeks validation to exist and so many of us constantly compensate in life with thoughts of ambition, accomplishment, and stature. When you were young, you were without the truth of who you really are, so you went to seek reference points from those around you. "If I don't know myself as this, then I must be that." And so an identity was born—an Ego, an opposite of truth.

The Ego, as we call it, represents the sum total of a person's belief systems—the persona that a person sees as themself.

The Ego, as it is derived from false beliefs, is the opposite of what is real, of a person's very nature. It is all things that are untrue. It is hatred and fear. It is that voice inside us that compels us to hide, justify, or defend. It is that very part of us that has us see ourselves as separate and small—the opposite of what is true.

Your Ego clouds the truth of who you are, what you are

capable of, leaving you with a totally inaccurate view of how to achieve happiness and a fulfilling life. It seeks an identity by drawing on comparison.

The Ego ages the physical body—it is truth that restores youth.

To conquer the influence of your Ego, you need to know it as just a belief system, a connection to something other than you. An Ego survives because it is reinforced. Ego feeds on the food of comparison, an identity derived from 'have-nots' rather than 'atone-with-alls.'

Your identity forms the basis of every decision you make. The Ego effectively traps you into thinking you are somebody else for the period that you are human. This serves an overall purpose, but only when you are aware that the Ego exists.

The dangers of having your Ego decide who you are in every moment is that you end up living a life of opposites. Your identity keeps showing up in life until you no longer believe it is real, until you are no longer attached to a particular reality or parts thereof. Enlightenment is the unfolding of your true identity— one of immeasurable abilities and talents—the non-Ego.

We often resist growth as we feel it invalidates our past decisions. In truth, we are the personification of growth—resistance is futile!

Your Ego is the loudest of your thoughts, because it is the most familiar. You live out your life predominantly from your Ego, programmed that way from birth by the beliefs and Ego of your parents, until you learn to distinguish the more subtle frequency of that inner knowing—your True Self's voice, your intuition.

Because the inner knowing is soft and gentle, it is given far less authority than that which you perceive most often. In stillness you access more of your True Self, rather than just your belief systems.

Many people are afraid to shine, avoiding ruffling feathers or having someone feel inadequate. Imagine you are in a pitch black room with those around you. When you dim your light, neither you nor they can see. When you shine brightly, you all can see. So shine brightly for all to see!

Your thoughts of control, domination, needing approval, recognition, and the need for attention from others are all expressions of the Ego. The frequency of the Ego is always outward-focused, meaning it seeks an identity and therefore reassurance from others.

The True Self, being the opposite of your Ego, needs nothing! It is inward, helping you to see yourself as whole, complete, needing nothing from others, interconnected, and All Knowing.

Speak your truth to others

41

Your Ego creates an alternate reality, one entirely unsuitable for you. It is a parallel universe where up is down, good is bad and love is fear.

Have you ever noticed that the minute you finally get what you have always wanted you start striving for the next level? The Ego's appetite is insatiable, a recipe for unhappiness. To try and please its ever-expanding wants is getting you into trouble as an individual and all of us on a global scale.

This reality can be witnessed everywhere! Look how much of what is real and true (nature) has been replaced with Ego-attempts at greatness—skyscrapers, roads, shopping malls and whole cities are covered in cement and tar. Humanity's lack of inward self-love has led to seeking outward recognition. You suffer for this, as does the planet and all its inhabitants.

What feeds your Ego are those things you do not need. What your Ego latches on to is subject to a person's insecurities—anything to fill a void of not being enough in your current state.

Ego-triggers vary per person and per culture. Some common triggers include: being challenged to expand who you see yourself to be, being shown up for being wrong, drugs, drama, what's in fashion, advertising, signage, war and violence, pornography, public nudity, comparison to others, the need to keep up, looking good, being the best and so on ... anything that leaves

---

Be first who you think everyone else should be

you with a sense of incompleteness, inadequacy. "I'm not enough," or "I need to be seen as more, or have more," is an indication that your Ego is in the driver's seat.

These triggers bring your belief system—your Ego—to the forefront, like being possessed by what is false. This is often accompanied by feelings of stress, anxiety, fear and general unpleasantness. This is the worst space to make decisions from, as it represents opposites. Any decisions made from opposites—from Ego—lead to the opposite of what makes you happy and fulfilled.

This overall inadequacy plays out in one of two ways. For some, their Ego has them feel inadequate, while for others their Ego lives through feelings of superiority. Either space creates decisions with unsatisfying outcomes.

Most believe wholeheartedly what the Ego is having them feel. The usual Ego taunts include: "I am a failure," or "Nobody wants me," or "I am misunderstood or misrepresented." Or conversely: "No one does as good a job as me," or "I know more about everything than anybody else," and so on.

Your Ego knows exactly how to bring you to your knees every time. It is a Consciousness, a form of intelligence that draws on your inadequacies.

Depression is the most direct symptom of believing what your Ego says about you.

Your Ego lives through your lack of awareness to it. Become aware—shine the light of awareness on your Ego—and it loses all its power over you. But, be playful about it—to be anything else would be coming from Ego once again.

It is the feelings you experience that are the giveaways as to what space you are coming from—your True Self or your Ego. When you come from Ego, you will experience unease and tightness in the body, feeling you need to defend your position, justify your actions, or lash out at someone. When you return to your True Self space in stillness, you will be left feeling calm and centered. Stillness is the opposite of Ego chatter.

Most people do not realize how easily their Ego is destroying what was going to be a great life. They get a feeling in their body and let that dictate their decisions. So many people confuse the messages and feelings of the Ego for intuition. On the contrary, intuition is clarity, a knowing that there is a more suitable or appropriate path for you. Being overridden with fear is Ego.

Soul Space is where purpose exists,
Ego Space is where chaos exists

Your intuition is not fear-based; it never uses fear as a means of steering you in the right direction. The less attachments you have to your reality, the less you believe to be real, the less your Ego can thrive. Clear your limiting beliefs to end the nightmare of your Ego.

People's biggest fear in moving forward is:
"What do I stand to lose?" Is this not an odd fear
for people who are seeking MORE for their life?

Do not let your Ego win, it is simply there to show you
what is not real, so you will learn to walk the path of
what IS real!

Why Is It That So Many Believe What Everyone Else Believes In?
Is It Working?

So many people are afraid to stand alone. They will sell
out their own joy and happiness, spanning an entire
lifetime, rather than face ridicule or persecution—the
ultimate in rejection. What they do not realize is that
persecution is just other people mirroring back the
same fears, because in the end all anybody wants is love.

The truth, however, is that love on the outside begins
with love on the inside. One cannot experience from
someone else what one cannot see within oneself. So
love yourself entirely first and your fears of rejection
will fade to nothing.

You do not need outside approval, just inside approval

Are Our Reactions The Truth?

What makes you angry, offended, feel rejected, or feel the need to defend and prove yourself? Are you reacting to a real threat? Your reactions stem from past experiences, where certain events had you believe something ugly about yourself. These events are triggered when something in the present resembles an event from the past in some way.

> *Your reactions are your responses to past events. Clear the past emotion and you clear future reactions.*

Your beliefs about yourself and your reality are being called into being (in truth, they are wanting to be healed, shown up for being false), but instead you fight off these feelings during your reaction space by yelling, crying, arguing, blaming others—avoiding them at all costs.

Instead, recognize your reactions as a trigger for growth—that your Ego is active and that it is time to repair past memories. In a space of reaction, where you feel anger, Frustration, or an intense surge of emotion, know immediately that this is not your True Self, but the opposite—your Ego. Before talking, giving a response, or making a decision, clear your Ego! No action of any kind should be made from this space, no matter how frustrated or upset you are. Any response, any decision made within this 'opposite' space will create the opposite outcome to what you truly desire for yourself. Furthermore, don't take it personally if others lash out at you from this space. Know that what they say from their Ego is not the truth!

Be Ego-free and you will set your life free!

Each reaction brings your awareness closer to seeing your True Self.

Is The Material World Helping or Hindering?

"I am spinning out of control—an insatiable appetite for more, a one-off fix for everyone's woes."

Where does it all stem from?

Our acquisitions are an attempt to fill a void that is having you feel incomplete in your very nature. You long for more things because you long for more within yourself. The trouble is nothing will ever permanently fill that void, because everything added is on top of something missing to begin with. Sooner or later the next new thing arrives and you will be immediately drawn to that as well.

Underneath all of this longing is actually a longing for self-love and self-acceptance. To know yourself as a perfect being will end this gluttony for material possessions.

Forgiveness is something you do, not something you get

A perfectly whole being wants only their needs, letting go of heavy purchases to remain light and nimble. Have you ever noticed how your purchases bog you down? A sense of heaviness, of being tied down accompanies them. This is because they do not take away your problems, but rather bury your problems even deeper. Many would rather hide behind their possessions, running away from the root cause of their unhappiness.

The solution is to first look within yourself to see what voids exist there. You are just reacting to beliefs about who you were taught to be—not who you really are. You keep running from these beliefs as if they are the truth, but they are not; they are just mind-made conclusions without facts. It is important to look at these prior to wasting your money on the next acquisition, before it too clutters your life even further.

Why Do We Crave To Look Good?

Many people are obsessed with keeping up an appearance—both to themselves and to others. This is fueled by many things, but primarily your beliefs about not being enough, loveable, or worthwhile. So you feel you need certain purchases, certain status, certain accomplishments, and so on—your Ego insisting you are nothing without these acquisitions.

The truth is you are everything—with or without these in your life.

Comparison to others is how your identity (Ego) keeps itself alive. This identity enjoys you feeling inadequate as a means of keeping you in your comfort zone.

Getting to know this person—the real you—is the trick. It is called the journey of enlightenment, to realize yourself as separate from your beliefs about yourself. In a space of enlightenment, you see yourself as needing nothing else—you are truly one with everything, so the need to add to yourself is eradicated.

Looking good keeps you feeling bad.

If you feel the urge to look a particular way to uphold an image, the solution is simple:

Imagine the opposite experience of looking good, the failure you are fearing. Go there in your mind as if it has already happened, stare the experience you dread in the eyes, sit with the emotions until they subside, getting through to the other side. Do not run from your feelings, just sit and be with them. They will not stay long, and soon you will be on the other side of these fears, better equipped to move forward more freely.

Money is attracted to self-belief, self-love and Soul Purpose

Why Do Some People Push All Our Buttons?

We see ourselves in others. The more you see what you like about yourself in others, the more you like that person. Conversely, the more you see what you do not like about yourself in others, the less you like that person. This becomes a challenge when communicating or establishing a relationship. If you are unable to resolve those parts within yourself, the relationship suffers. The clearer you are about who you are, the more free-flowing a relationship can be.

Each person reminds you of something within your past—an experience, an emotion, or a person. How you dealt with that past event comes back for healing in how it shows up in the present. Each reaction is a past event coming up for resolution. The more you clear the past, the clearer and more refined your future becomes. It takes resolving the past to end past patterns. It takes knowing yourself in this new light to make new decisions. It takes new decisions to create new and bigger futures.

Allow the past to resurface—
your reactions are a blessing in disguise.

Is It Right To Relive The Past?

Do you obsess over your childhood years? No. Do you obsess over how last week was spent? No. So one might ask: Why do you obsess over events that happened 2000 years ago? Why do you obsess over wars that were fought decades ago? What does this do for us? Do you think it prevents it from occurring again? Is it healing for those involved to relive these events over and over again?

The answer is no, it simply perpetuates past decisions into the present moment. A strange phenomenon exists to dwell on our past. It is curious that we leave the present at all. Reliving the past distracts from the present; and it is in the present that decisions about the future are made.

When you are stuck in the past, the decisions made for the future come from the past. If you live in the past, you fail to see the opportunities of the present.

If you live in the past and make no attempt to forgive yourself and others, to see the error of your ways and the very thinking that created these experiences, reliving the past actually dooms you to repeat the same mistakes. What you still believe is repeated in your current experience of life.

Empty your vessel of beliefs, make room for what is real

The past happened because of who you were at that time, not who you are today. If you allow yourself free trips to the past, who you are now starts to become who you were back then.

Be careful what you are handing down from one generation to the next. Is it hate or love? Is it anger or acceptance?

It is important to clear your own beliefs so as not to inflict them on your children, dooming the next generation to do the same all over again.

What Lessons Can Be Learned From Structured Belief Systems? Does Religion Have The Answers?

For a structured belief system to be in someone's highest good, it must be empowering!

Many religions disguise the disempowerment their belief system creates by having their followers believe that they come to this earth empty, needing to prove themselves to 'God' (or someone else) in order to be worthy and valid.

This false belief system sustains the religion, as it creates dependency on the system rather than creating self-

empowered beings. It creates followers instead
of masters.

Many religions claim to be about spiritual development.
Yet so many have actually gone about spiritual
development in the exact opposite way to how spiritual
development works. Spiritual growth and evolution
begins with self-belief, not self-doubt.

It comes from seeing oneself as whole and complete
(the True Self), to believe "I am one with all that Is."
This is the space that syncs both the Conscious and
Subconscious Minds to the infinite wisdom that is the
spiritual realm.

Instead, many religions have their followers begin life
starting with self-doubt, by having them need to earn
their place on Earth, with rituals and sacrifices, diets
and harm to the body. Beginning life with self-doubt
has a person feel they are inadequate, not enough, and
not lovable. Living without nourishment and positive
reinforcement leads to the very socially destructive
behaviors that religions claim they are here to correct.
Some of these behaviors include self-abuse, unnecessary
ambition, hate toward others who are seen to have more
or be different, divorce, alcohol and drug abuse, greed,
and so on. All these dysfunctions come from self-doubt.

The truth is that direction or intuition comes from
within. True self-belief fosters strength, courage, and
mastery over one's life. Purpose comes from within, not
sourced from another.

Watch yourself grow up

Is religion creating leaders or followers? For a religion to truly serve its purpose, self-belief must be top of its agenda. Empowered or disempowered? That is the question!

Question: What belief system reaches enlightenment fastest? Answer: The one that sees no other to be inferior to it.

How Do We Grow Fast?

Looking at the 'hard stuff' in your life allows success in much faster than not looking. The faster you cleanse yourself of what holds you back, the sooner you get what you really want!

Have you been told you are not enough? People subconsciously use their biggest fears as their biggest insults. If someone in your life has had you feel inadequate, it is because their darkest fear, behind all the facades, is that they themselves are inadequate. Instead of confronting these fears, some people attempt to squash others so they themselves look adequate, even great, in comparison.

My Reflections

Why Did The Concept Of 'Beliefs' Present Itself In Our Lives?

My wife Sonja and I had been working with people, teaching them how to access their All Knowing Self (Universal Intelligence), and what we found was that many had a natural predisposition toward learning this ability while some struggled immensely. I asked myself what the difference is between these people. It came through that at the heart of all talents and abilities lie the beliefs we hold about those talents and abilities. Having this realization, we probed deeper, asking our All Knowing Self: "What is the most efficient way to change our Subconscious Belief systems?" What we were shown was profoundly simple, quick, and easy for everyone. It is still the very same methodology we teach in all our courses.

Why Did The Concept Of The 'Ego' Present Itself For Our Understanding And Teachings?

We know that there are always two sides to every coin. We can see it almost everywhere, but what we didn't quite understand was what was generating negativity within people, what was really the source of extremes on Earth, of violence and aggression? What we discovered was amazing! We were shown that at the beginning, when human beings were introduced onto this earth, the process required the inclusion of two energy systems, both a light energy and a dark energy— exact opposites. This created 'free will', so to speak—the choice for a human being to live out their life by either choosing a light energy or a dark energy to draw on, for making decisions and experiencing life.

Truth 2

Thought Is REAL ...

"We are all Conscious beings. Like a still pond mirroring what is above, Consciousness is what was first. Thought creates, thought is self-aware, and thought is everywhere."

Treat others as you would like to be treated

How Did It All Begin?

This is a story about all of us making our way on the journey we call life ...

Once upon a time, there was a bright white light that flooded the entire Universe. All that could be seen was this light, no one and nothing else existed. But there was something unique about this light ... it was self-aware ... it knew it existed ... it could think.

As it began to know itself as this light, over time it became bored with itself and decided that a new experience was necessary. And so, at the speed of thought, this light subdivided itself into streams of color—like a rainbow spanning the width and breadth of the entire Universe.

Beautiful rich colors, as far as could be seen. Deep purples, magnificent reds, yellow bright and bubbly, majestic blues and oranges, natural green, and so on ... Each color possessed the same qualities of the light that came before. The colors too were self-aware, able to think.

Over time, these colors learned who they were, and so it was time to become more, to divide once again into even more colors. Now, deeper purples existed, richer blues, a greater variety of greens, and so on. A sky made of brilliant bright color, spanning the whole Universe.

This experience continued, until such a time when the colors reconnected more and more with their true nature, as creators themselves. So they began experimenting with each other, seeing what else could be created, what new variety of themselves could be experienced. What new shades, patterns and textures could be created for the rest of itself to experience.

The colors experimented together, mixing and matching, experiencing themselves in all manner of brilliance. It was glorious; for the first time, color existed in our Universe.

Once they became bored with this, they realized a new experience was missing. What if there was an opposite of themselves, what if an opposite could also be experienced? This was a breakthrough in thinking, to realize one could exist as itself and as an opposite.

And, as before, through the magic of intention (directed thought), they divided once again, creating an opposite of light—creating darkness. This, being a new version of themselves, created a more whole experience. Light gave birth to dark, and now, for the first time ever in the Universe, contrast existed.

Opposite existed. It was magical! An entirely new concept had been born from thought.

Contrast gave birth to a later realization—that is, "How can I be one without the other? If I am one, I must simultaneously also be the other. Both are part of my new color spectrum and so we are one ... there is no separation."

Time passed, new experiences arose and one realization after another occurred. A giant leap in awareness was

---

We are a young civilization with much growth ahead

happening. The Universe could experience itself in so many ways never previously imagined, simultaneous and unique all at once. A heightened level of Consciousness was being born into existence—deep self-awareness.

The colors and their opposites began to ask more and more questions: What else could exist other than myself? How much is possible right now? I know myself as many shades of the one color, I have even experienced myself as light and dark, but what else could I exist as? How else could I experience my reality?

A realization struck, one of huge significance: The more I am, the more I can experience myself in so many different ways. The more I see myself to be, the bigger my experience becomes!

What followed changed the Universe forever. An immense flash of inspiration took place, creating a perception of physical dimension, a new version of thought in motion. This new physical reality scattered itself throughout wide open spaces, forming 'like-minded' particles joining together, and so on. The Universe now mirrored itself as thought and its physical reality. For the first time, opposites existed in thought and now also in physical density.

These building blocks of the entire Universe all had one thing in common: To seek more from itself, to be more for itself, to know itself as more!

And so, thought and intention underpinned all physical matter, an intelligence that was both self-aware and all one. This new intelligence spanned every corner of the Universe. An All Knowing was born, both physical and non-physical. As all was connected, all aspects and all manifestations could sustain themselves from this one collective pool of intelligence, a web of knowledge that could govern physical reality—a safeguard to ensure balance and harmony was becoming accessible for all.

With non-physical intelligence—Consciousness now interwoven within all physical matter—this All Knowing could continue to expand and discover new frontiers, thinking and creating—'thought' being the foundation of all creations.

But a new discovery was on the horizon, a new type of contrast, one never encountered before. An opposite in so many ways ... 'life' was beginning to be conceived. How would I experience myself directly? How would I know who I am, if I were alive?

And so the Universe pooled its far-reaching intelligence and began designing physical life in a myriad of ways, from the complex grand to the simple miniature and everything in between—matter so dense it would be virtually unaware of itself once it was born.

In support of this new idea, a layering process continued for many, many years—layers of physical reality being created to support the next and so on. Like a background to a future foreground.

After a while, this intelligent matter wanted more from life, a unique experience where what one believed would be that which one conceived. A complex reality with coinciding belief systems, every imagination

---

Release those who do not support you

61

created and intertwined with another. What if I forgot myself every time, needing to remember myself again and again? What if I could see through unique eyes each time, with new skills, new friends, new challenges, drawing on both the assets of the physical and the non-physical Universe? What would I paint then?

And so, the human being evolved, birthed into the world unaware, unknowing, but departing the physical world once again All Knowing. And so it began, the physical human experience, with an exterior of flesh and bone and pure Consciousness underneath to roam the physical plane. Five physical senses to indulge, a mind unlimited in its nature and, additionally, a sixth sense that is your nature.

The Human Being

Pure All Knowing at the start,
And forever, if kept close to the heart.
A Universe within,
Who could create anything.
See yourself as new, a glowing light,
That without fear can be so bright.
That is you—the truth within,
An All Knowing being!

How Does Our Universe Really Work?

Welcome to a quantum leap in your intelligence, a leap in human Consciousness, the next phase of your evolution—you seeing yourself as pure Consciousness, as pure thought.

It has been thought that the Universe is simply energy, but that is not quite accurate. It is more aptly described as conscious awareness, or thought.

Everything is thought. Your physical body is thought, the earth is thought and the Universe is thought.

Hard to imagine? Well, your imagination is also thought—so keep up!

What you 'think' is a substance that you belong to. It is not from your brain; it is more accurate to say your brain is from thought. You harness thoughts to think, but thought is not dependent on you to exist.

Try to imagine everything being the substance of thought, like your Consciousness contained within your body. Everything you perceive as the physical Universe also carries self-awareness—Consciousness.

Consciousness is intelligent matter and holds many answers to many questions. To understand the Universe, equate it to a physical person—it helps to understand the whole picture. You have conscious awareness throughout your physical being, as does the Universe. You are the micro of the macro, a perfect representation.

Are We The Only Ones Having Beliefs?

In Truth 1, we examined the concept: what you believe is what you experience. Thought and belief go hand in hand, but you as a human being are not the only one drawing on thought, nor are you the only one holding beliefs, for that matter. All Consciousness is capable of belief.

If you believe yourself to be one way, you experience yourself in that way, as that thought. Likewise, the earth is thought knowing itself as a water planet ... and so on and so forth.

This intelligent energy takes many forms, ultimately forming a Universal Field connecting all things to the source of all thought. As such, as everything is thought and thought is information, infinite knowledge makes up your landscape. All thought is connected, interrelated, and so all thought is All Knowing.

Your thoughts, on the other hand, are limited only by how you think about yourself and this reality, because a belief is a thought and, as such, you experience it.

But the absolute thought is pure All Knowing. Many of your thoughts are you projecting a false reality—the reality created by your beliefs—that undermines your true possibility.

Your evolution is this false reality dissolving; it is you seeing beyond your own belief systems.

As everything is thought, fields of thought sweep across your land, containing infinite wisdom, full of unlocked know-how and ancient secrets that wait to be rediscovered. These fields contain more than human thought—they also contain versions of your reality previously unexperienced by humanity. These fields contain limitless information on any conceivable topic, and topics that are yet to be conceived.

How Is It Possible?

As thought or pure Consciousness, your 'scenery,' your world, your Universe is not static. It is not dead or inanimate. On the contrary—your scenery, your physical world IS you. It is another manifestation of you, as is your physical body. You are born of thought; the world is too, as are all inhabitants on Earth, and in essence everything is connected through thought.

Thought is the truth—
everything else is just a reflection.

Your physical world is, in its simplest manifestation, a hologram made from thought. You, being a thinking being, are created by thought and connected to it. You then play a large role in affecting your surrounding

---

Live your higher purpose, discover it now!

world just by thinking. The physical world is like putty that responds to thought, your feelings, your words and more obviously your actions. It is an interactive playground of self-discovery. It is like a movie set, a stage that mirrors you and evolves and changes as you do. It is designed this way very purposefully, of course, to show you how big or how small you see yourself to be.

It is your emotionally charged thoughts that shape, cause, create, alter and modify your physical world. As alluded to earlier, your physical world refers to both your physical body and your physical surroundings; after all, they are inseparable from your thoughts.

Have you ever noticed any of these?:

∞ Being in a great mood and everyone seems to be smiling at you?

∞ Starting the day angry and then experiencing "bad luck," a "bad mood," or "accidents" happening throughout the day?

∞ Receiving or experiencing the one thing you have dreamed of and wished for all your life?

∞ Experiencing a mishap or disaster that you have feared all your life? (This could be anything from a partner having an affair to going bankrupt, or a robbery.)

∞ Experiencing the weather being perfect—or disastrous—on a specific day of the year where people want it to be great to celebrate something, or where people hold a belief that it is always sunny/ miserable that day?

Affecting your environment through thought can be a harsh reality for some and liberating and freeing to others. The fact that your emotionally charged thoughts create or destroy can be seen as a licence to create the life and world of your dreams. It means you are at cause rather than at effect in your world, learning the discipline of your thoughts and behaviors. Many fight against this truth by blaming a deity, being angry, hurting others and even hurting themselves—refusing to take responsibility for their own life.

Thought is everything. Thought 'energy' is the substance that the entire Universe is made of. If you release the notion of physicality and embrace a world made of thought, then you begin to see physical boundaries melt like candle wax. Infinite possibilities become available.

Everything you see, feel, touch, taste, smell or hear is thought.

This is the most empowering realization. It literally means if you can think it, you can experience it ... if you allow yourself to.

So, where did all this thought come from? The answer to this conundrum is far simpler than what you would think. You need to consider that your perceptions of time and space are not really very accurate. You currently see a linear existence of past, present, and future, when in fact it is all happening right now. This

---

Do not let other people's fears of what is possible dictate your decisions.

can be difficult to allow in, but it is not important right now, so take your time with this one. The source of thought is the same as it has always been. The source of thought now, as always, is simply Consciousness itself— a field of electricity spanning the Universe as a whole. Everything that ever was, and everything that ever will be, is thought—Consciousness expanding, All Knowing.

Thought started it all and now it is continuing its self-exploration and expression as YOU!

The birth of the Universe as we know it was the birth of thought knowing itself in a multitude of ways. Thought preceded the creation of the Universe. First there was thought, then there was light, then there was life.

Thought is not indistinguishable from itself.
If it is 'in existence,' it is thought.

Anything that is in the physical realm started as a thought. Consider as you read that you are witnessing billions of years of thought, thoughts being added, of thoughts being transformed, and then of thoughts materializing into denser physical experience.

Thought is what is true. Physical is the illusion!

The best way to comprehend this notion is to interrogate the previous assumptions you have been carrying about the word 'thought.' The term has been long used to describe an activity of mankind, or an activity exhibited by some species in the animal kingdom.

To many (in fact, to nearly every human being), thought is what you do. It is an intangible activity that precedes an action or feeling. You have a thought: *I am hungry*, so you act and feed yourself ... and so on.

The word—or concept—'thought,' has been vandalized over countless years of usage. Its original application has unfortunately been lost ... until now.

If you relate to a concept or definition the same way over and over again, you cease questioning its definition or purpose. You also, if you ever did, stop questioning its origins.

In some cases, when a word loses its true meaning, there are few consequences. However, in this case, more serious side-effects have occurred. The word 'thought' used to stand for a process by which life was created or destroyed. If you think about it now, you can see this practically, because either your thoughts (especially today) create (positive thoughts), or destroy (negative thoughts), or are neutral (i.e. they are non-emotionally backed thoughts).

One can say enlightenment was largely extinguished by loss of proper word usage—the forgotten meaning behind the word 'thought.' As the word usage shifted to an elementary level, so too did mankind's understanding of planet Earth and the Universe.

This word 'thought' actually holds the answer to all of life's biggest mysteries. From pain-free births to what happens after death, cures for all illnesses, workable

---

Be honest with yourself, lies hurt the body

financial systems, the rebalancing of greed, sex, warfare, to the fountain of youth.

As such, when you hear the word 'thought,' you can only comprehend it in terms of something you do or do not do.

Imagine for a minute that thought is actually you—not something you do, but something you are. Imagine that rather than generating thoughts, you actually experience thoughts, that this is the fundamental purpose behind your brain—to extract and experience thought.

Are We Using Our Brain Correctly?

The true purpose of the brain has also been confused over the years. We have confused the memory function with the decision-making function, meaning that we spend too much time recalling past thoughts, rather than tuning into new, innovative and fresh thoughts.

By constantly and stubbornly rehashing past thoughts, we limit our world largely to what we have already experienced, or believe can be experienced. The impact of this is our stagnation and the stagnation of our species, as we continue to repeat the same old patterns. This is why our evolution as a species is so slow.

***Using your brain to extract new
or 'virgin thought' is its true purpose,
not to draw on old thoughts.***

Exceptional thinkers have already been accepted, or acknowledged, for using a higher percentage of their brain (or, better stated, all of their brain). That is where true genius stems from—proper brain use. Not a better brain, just better brain usage. Like all major organs in the body, the brain is harnessing 'food' inputs to create and experience. The body utilizes what is external to it to survive and prosper, as does your brain. It is how the Universe is designed, having 'beings' very efficiently harness common 'food sources' rather than each 'being' carrying around their own.

Consider that your brain is sensing the thought frequencies of everything that it interacts with. It senses thought waves of words, of people, of sunlight, of the atmosphere, of thoughts behind words, and so on. <u>Your brain is, as is the rest of you, a recording and receiving station for thought frequencies. Your brain is like an antenna, just like a radio, capable of 'tuning in' to different thoughts rather than radio stations.</u> This is why you can walk into a room and feel the 'vibe'—vibe obviously being some sort of vibration. It also explains why two inventors on either side of the planet can access the same idea at the same time. Many currently unexplained phenomena on Earth are explained in this way.

Why is this important?

Your brain certainly has the capacity to re-order, sort, and produce various combinations of 'known information'—your past thoughts and experiences —but when it does this it ceases to interact with its ecosystem, potentially creating thoughts that do not benefit the collective. 'Stand-alone' thinking, thinking that is not drawing on the field of intelligence, creates decisions potentially harmful to ecology (as an individual or as a collective), as these decisions come from insufficient information.

Stand-alone thinking creates short-term solutions but long-term problems.

Classic examples include: fossil fuel usage, overuse of plastics, utilizing landfill as a solution to garbage removal and so on.

Our ecosystems were created through drawing on this field of intelligence, and, in fact, this intelligence is the ecosystem. As such, all ecosystems—be they the ecosystem of your body or of the planet—depend on you extracting the right solutions to your challenges from this collective intelligence. When this replaces stand-alone thinking, we will begin to contribute to nature instead of destroying it.

There is a current of energy—a field of electricity —that sustains all life. It carries information that keeps us alive. You belong to it, you are it, and you were made because of it. Your purpose is to reconnect to it. It is the source of your genius and your inspiration.

On a personal note, if all you do is make your brain reconfigure combinations of old thoughts, then you will never live a new life. The same thoughts give you the same life, with only minor variation. New thoughts, or new perceptions of life, equal a new way of living.

The only true way to live a new life is to allow totally new concepts into your brain. Remember, your old thoughts got you where you are today. If you want new experiences, you need to start creating new thoughts. The way to do this is to use your brain to tune in to all intelligence, into All Knowing.

Use your brain like an antenna, scouring the Universe for what is new—then you will live anew!

Dollar For Dollar

What you see is what you get. In order to help you grow and evolve, your reality is based on mirror reflection. What this means is that who you see yourself to be is reflected back at you inside your experience of life.

Do not lie in order to hide your true feelings

Dollar for dollar, the Universe says. I will match your experience dollar for dollar, for just how big you are being about your life right now.

The experiences you have are a direct reflection of how big you see yourself—or how small for that matter.

The bigger you see yourself to be, the bigger the experiences you will have. If you have small thoughts about finances, you will experience small amounts of finance. If you think big in relationships and how great they can be, you will experience just that.

Start practicing having big thoughts and you will start having big experiences!

Some big thoughts include:

∞ I am worthy of greatness

∞ I am pure creativity

∞ I am the creative force in my life

∞ I am connected to all things

∞ There is infinite intelligence available to me

∞ Everything I see is a part of me

∞ Loving myself is reflected in my world back to me

Are We All We Think We Are?

This field of electricity that permeates all physical matter lies within you, as a personalized Universal Consciousness for you to access.

It links you with All Knowing and all human beings, to the specific intelligence necessary to play out your role in life.

Some Call It Your True Self

I am you, you are me,
Together we see everything!
Think of me as the Universe inside,
Your True Self or Soul, the ultimate guide!
I am pure intelligence,
Unconstrained by your belief systems.
I am a part of you that never dies,
A part of you that need not lie.
See yourself as me,
And you will have many victories.
I am you, the real you,
Not the false version that you once knew.

Look after nature and it will look after you

Over the years, through pain and grief,
My thoughts have remained hidden under your beliefs.
I am but a whisper, I'm part of your skin,
A field of intelligence, something to believe in.
Nothing is separate, nothing is small,
You are part of this Universe as a whole.
Some call me True Self, The Truth; others the Soul,
It's time for human beings to see themselves as whole.
I am the source of inspiration,
I am what is called your intuition.
Draw on me for matters large or small,
And together everyone on Earth can live tall.
This is the era of the True Self, of self-realization.
It's not an option, but your evolution,
You can no longer deny that your True Self exists,
For without it, life will be miffed.
From the dreams in your head,
To the genius that wakes you from your bed,
To the coincidences that you think are eerie,
To the messages from your friends that seem freaky.
Your True Self is behind your life,
The architect of your divine rights.
Draw on it—your True Self—
To repair your life, remove the spell.
It's up to you, to choose to be tall,
You are not separate, but a part of the all.
Your mind has tricked you into believing what's untrue,
Now it's time to access the real, infinite you!

Let Me Go Deeper

I am thought, this world you see,
Everything here is a part of me.
Imagine the Universe you see,
But imagine it as a big brain—you see?
The planets and the stars above
Are simply a projection of what matters above.
All you see, trees and birds in ecstasy,
Are me, living so happily.
Thought is real, the physical is not,
Your mind deciphers through who you are not.
Everything you can see,
Everything is my electricity.
Thought governs all; it belongs to you all,
Like a giant library that knows it all.
Your brain that is within you
Can plainly see the Universe inside of you.
Every inch of you
Carries the Universe, it's true.
All matter, dense or light, is thought,
Experiencing itself to know what's right.
But all thought is self-aware,
Nothing is ever bare!
It's all intelligence, a library sublime—
One you can access to live a life so divine.
Move beyond your thoughts
To something new.
Switch over to your All Knowing self,

Cleanse your body of others' negative thoughts

And be prepared for something else.
I am the All Knowing contained in your veins,
A Soul, a light that has no pain.
I'm the whisper in your head,
The genius who speaks in bed,
The knowing your intuition tells,
That vast opposite of what you'd call hell.
Realize this: intelligence is not in the brain,
But exists everywhere, no matter your pain.
The Universe is not random,
But rather thought in amalgam.
Nothing is without intelligence.
Everything is on purpose.
It's time you human beings saw
Your own divine purpose.
Thought is real, that's the truth,
The architect of reality, that's living proof.
Thought creates, thought designs,
All the animals in your barn.
Nature is thought, it is true,
The same intelligence is inside of you.
Call me your Soul, your True Self,
I am what is real, not just your Self.
I am Consciousness inside you,
Not your beliefs, they are untrue.
Very few know who I am and so they fail,
I am the designer of the life you all hail.
I whisper through your thoughts so you can hear me,
It's time to be more, it's time to see me.
I am your dreams, your inspiration too,
It's time more of you call upon me too.

How Does The Universe Reveal Itself To Us?

In many ways:

<u>The Human Being is the Universe personified.</u> You are Consciousness, embodied in physical form. You think and you create exactly how the Universe works. The physical is a reflection of the thought (your thoughts). Healthy thoughts equal a healthy physicality. The outer Universe is a reflection of the inner Universe, they are one and the same.

<u>Life on Earth mirrors the vast realms of life throughout the Universe,</u> each species on Earth playing a different role, harmonizing and maintaining a balanced ecosystem. So it is throughout the Universe, teeming with life.

<u>The colors of a prism show how first thought envisaged what could be next,</u> separating itself into multiple streams of color—the very basis of life as you know it. One concept layered on top of another concept, making the next possible. Thought preceded new thought and so on.

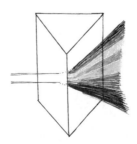

The Solar System has all planets revolving around a bright source of light that gives life, fueling a planetary ecosystem. You too have a sun within you—your True Self—which functions your ecosystem, attempting to maintain its balance as best as possible.

Hence your intuition and the aches and pains in your body, steering you back to your Life Purpose path!

A dandelion gives you a great insight into the very shape of the physical Universe, a projection of thought. New seeds go on to create new flowers, like new thoughts go on to create new thoughts from themselves, the building blocks of the Universe.

Why Are We Here?

Each corner of the Universe has an ecosystem, a level of intelligence contributing to the whole (entire Universe) by creating a particular reality. This reality underpins other, further realities, making a new experience at a higher level possible. For example, in school, First grade supports the teaching and reality of second grade, which then supports the teaching and reality of third grade ...

Within this reality, mankind plays a vital role in equipping the Soul or True Self with the necessary tools and abilities—the building blocks of creation—like a training manual on the job, to allow them to move onto the next layers of the evolution, which is to create life and worlds by themselves.

The lifetime of a human being is the training ground for balance and equilibrium (i.e. the building blocks of the entire Universe). A human being's world or life experience is a subset, or miniature, of what a True Self is working towards. A human life is the model railway, if you like, with the True Self working toward creating an actual live working railway.

And so, it is essential that all human beings move toward True Self intelligence—All Knowing—to allow balance and equilibrium into their own life experience.

A human being's evolution and a True Self's evolution run in parallel. Both must embrace the larger aspect of themselves to experience themselves as whole!

Our outer Universe is a reflection of our inner Universe. What we believe in our inner Universe becomes our reality in the entire Universe.

How Do We See Clearly? Turn It Upside Down!

Things are not always as they appear; in fact, they rarely are. And, as many of us move into a phase of uncertainty, a new message is required. It is time for people to hear what they have been resisting for so long. We live in a topsy-turvy world, where up has become down and

---

Give only what brings you joy—no more, no less

down has become up. Many of us are no longer seeing clearly what our reality consists of, or should consist of, in terms of what is actually in our highest good.

What can we do?

To see the right way up, we need to turn our current views upside down—where money comes first and nature comes last. Where our imagination is unreal and our physical world our true reality—turn that upside down. We have all become so accustomed to our way of life that we have forgotten what the right way up even looks like. Let's explore:

∞ Where your physical body is all there is, and a Soul is not real—turn it upside down!

∞ Where movie and sports stars are highly paid and enlightened teachers are expected to work for free—turn it upside down!

∞ Where you choose a hit of happiness first and fulfilment last—turn it upside down!

∞ Where your body comes last and your career comes first—turn it upside down!

∞ Where you think the stars and other planets are so far away, that you are alone—turn it upside down!

∞ Where you think living your Life Purpose will leave you poor and unhappy—turn it upside down!

∞ Where you think yelling at each other and your children works—turn it upside down!

∞ Where you think birthing and parenting has to be painful—turn it upside down!

- ∞ Where the military receive more money from governments than causes helping people to become more—turn it upside down!

- ∞ Where teachers create students instead of masters—turn it upside down!

- ∞ Where we believe it is necessary to add to ourselves to grow rather than removing what is false—turn it upside down!

One Plus One

1 + 1 = 2
But what if it weren't true?
Could it be something new?
What is real, what is true?
Is my reality me, or you?
Who drives it, who decides it?
I tell you now, it is me who designs it!
Could life become altogether new?
If it were up to me, I would live anew!
Take note and surely you will see
Everything I am is up to me.

How Do Our Thoughts Affect Us?

So far we have explored in brief how thoughts form the basis of the entire Universe. We have even looked at the birth of new thoughts and how they are a catalyst for growth and evolution. We have looked at the outer Universe being a reflection of the inner Universe.

But how does this translate to your physicality, your body, your health and well-being? Together we will explore the impact of thoughts on the physical body, on us as humans. There are so many unanswered questions relating to the cause and cure of illness, it is time we lay them to rest.

The Human Anatomy

So vastly misunderstood by so many all over the world, diet and nutrition is actually the smallest link in the chain for health and well-being, yet so much emphasis is placed on this input. Rather, the body is a vessel housing Consciousness, responding to thought about itself and thoughts from others.

The body believes in equilibrium and balance, peace not chaos. It responds to self-love and is crippled under self-hate. Its messages can be felt in how it reacts to thoughts, situations and people. It never lies, and always tells the truth.

The body is a repairing and self-sustaining organism. Nothing is impossible for it. With faith and trust in its capabilities, the body can do almost anything. It is built to last, currently over two hundred years in this climate, but cannot sustain a condition of self-hate— even slightly—for more than fifty years; after that it deteriorates severely.

The body's susceptibility to virus and infection stems from the beliefs that pump through its veins.

The greatest immunization is self-love,
that "I am impenetrable".

Self-hate opens the floodgates to all manner of breakdown. The body cannot sustain these thoughts for long. You must learn to cultivate a condition in the body of self-love, especially between the ages of two and four, to cement this reality, allowing the body to become far more resilient to illness and infection.

Thought is the truth! Everything—the symptoms in your body, the experiences in your life—is just a reflection. Seek the thoughts and you will find both cause and cure.

Our brain in Whole Brain State is able to diagnose all human ailments; it is the most sophisticated diagnostic equipment ever invented.

Let Us Go Deeper

To commence this journey, one needs to understand what the human body really is and what function it serves. Firstly, try to imagine that the human body is not YOU in your entirety. For many, their body is them, the beginning and the end, the vehicle, the personality, everything ... and when the body dies, they die with it.

This, thankfully, is not the case. Your body is neither the beginning nor the end. There is only the now, so

---

Live in nature as much as possible

consider no more beginnings to you and no more endings. You are in fact bigger than your body. Your body is simply and only the physical existence, or physical counterpart to a greater you. You are far beyond something finite. You neither live nor die, you simply exist. That is the real you, simply an aspect of this field of electricity.

Imagine a radio receiving center that monitors countless radio frequencies, that deciphers and interprets these frequencies and then reports back on the impact of such frequencies. This metaphor will get your mind pretty close to what the human body really is. The body is simply a highly sophisticated, highly capable recording and interpreting device. Its sole purpose is to experience. That is it. Nothing less and nothing more, just experience.

So what does it mean to experience? I am glad you asked. In this context, I use the word experience to encapsulate a multitude of tasks and activities. To experience really means to understand why. It means to assimilate physical and emotional sensations into some form of meaning or understanding.

For example, sipping on a cup of freshly made coffee will generate several physical and emotional sensations. You will feel the warmth on your lips, in your mouth, taste the coffee on your tongue, smell the coffee with your nose, then swallow the coffee with your throat and process the coffee with your stomach. Who would have thought drinking a cup of coffee could stimulate so much of you? And that is not even counting the aftereffects of drinking coffee as your body processes this input.

Without all those senses, you would not know the experience of drinking coffee in its fullest, most real expression. Here, you have experienced. You have also, through the experience, understood why to drink coffee or why not to drink coffee.

As a part of the All Knowing field of intelligence, you know of all things, but you do not know of it directly yourself, or what it means to you or others—the consequences, cause and effect, and so on.

You, as part of your experience, want to know something directly. You want to know why the experience has happened—was it worthwhile, was it destructive, what is the better way of doing things? By experiencing something directly for yourself, you can understand why. Why to experience it, why to continue the experience, or why to cease the experience. Your physical body (and physical reality) are but a means to allow the concept of direct experience to be possible. It allows you to see why or why not.

So, then, who is experiencing what? You know now that the body experiences. You know this directly as part of your daily life. You are constantly, in every second, experiencing. You experience pain, pleasure, love, joy, sadness, happiness, fear, anger, remorse, regret, jealousy, thrill, adrenalin rush … There are limitless experiences on Earth for us, countless combinations, permutations

---

Depression is severe self-hate... love yourself and you can be free and expressions. Why is the body here to experience all these things? If the body dies, what is the point of recording all this data and then dying? A great question!

Consider that the body is just a tool. As I alluded to earlier, the body is a receiving station. For who? The answer is simple, it is all for you. The real you—the limitless, infinite you. You in your rawest form are light. Put another way, you are pure energy, pure thought ... a non-physical amalgam of intelligent energy, as discussed. As this non-physical mass of energy, you have limited direct experience of what you know to be true. You know of many things, but you have not experienced them all for yourself directly in physical form.

Many people think they are here to do. But, despite what you will physically achieve or not achieve, you are here to experience, not do. Doing is just the facilitator for particular experiences. It is because of this, because of the prevalence of the doing, that people misconstrue the purpose of being here with doing rather than experiencing. Doing often precedes the being. But being is not dependent on doing. In fact, the purest form of being is in the absence of doing.

You use the body to have direct experience. The body is the fullest, most comprehensive way to do this. It sees, feels, hears, touches, smells, digests, swallows, breathes, plays, thinks, cries, angers, sweats, runs, walks, jumps, swims, grows, and much, much more. And you thought computers were clever creations! With this in mind, let us explore why you actually want direct experience with what you know.

Why Have A Direct Experience?

A direct experience is different from knowing an experience for one simple reason: to experience it directly shows you who you are in the face of it. How can one truly know who, what, or where they are without a reference point—without a mirror to reveal themselves?

If you are speaking to a friend and they tell you about a movie, you can only form a basic opinion about it. You could like it, hate it, love it, or never want to see it to begin with. But it is only when you are sitting in the cinema that you get the rush of adrenalin, feel afraid, feel touched, feel jealous, feel loss, or feel inspired. It is only when you are having a direct physical experience with the movie that you can fully experience how it affects you. It is only through being affected that you can gauge who you are in relation to what you have seen, heard, felt ... experienced.

In order to constantly grow, expand and realize your full potential, you need to see who you are in the face of 'life', or in the face of direct experience. While your body may only serve to experience, you have a much higher purpose or reason for existing. For now, it is important to understand the fundamentals.

Love yourself unconditionally

In summary:

∞ You are much larger than you can currently comprehend.

∞ You grow by continuously knowing who, what, and where you are.

∞ You know this by experiencing.

∞ The way you experience is by being and by direct encounter through the physical body.

∞ Direct physical experience acts as a mirror to who, what, and where you're at right now.

What Causes Illness And Disease?

The human body is a miraculous piece of the heavens. It is multi-tasking, multi-sensory and gives you a running commentary along the way. As you walk your path, navigating your way through life—creating and destroying— your body constantly shows up who you are being in your life. It shows this up in both inward experiences, in health and well-being, and in outward experiences of failure or fulfilment.

Your body continuously speaks to you, time and time again, in order to keep you healthy and prospering. But how do you know what it is saying? How can you listen if you do not know the cues, the prompts, or

---

Do not hold back who you are; and allow others to be who they are

the warning bells? How can you know what to do if the body speaks a language you were never taught? Your body actually speaks quite simply and in an unmistakable way. Your body speaks to you in feelings. Feelings are the language of the body. If you feel good, it is because you are doing good things (i.e. you are being in a way that has you think productive thoughts, has you speak productive words and has you do productive activities). You have a whole range of feelings that are used to communicate to you in a way you understand.

The problem to date has been the misinterpretation of these feelings.

For thousands of years, people have experienced various sensations in the body, from pain to pleasure and everything in between. The problem has been that people have not been aware enough to take responsibility for these sensations. Instead, people have blamed these sensations on everything but themselves. Feelings experienced in the body have been blamed or allocated to other people, or some other unexplained phenomenon. People have even continued to view these sensations or symptoms as random acts of nature.

Your body is a feedback mechanism that sends you messages in order to stay healthy and alive.

It alerts you with thirst when it requires hydration, with hunger when it requires sustenance, with fatigue when it needs rest. For every need, the body has a method of communicating back to us, to give it what it needs, now!

Unfortunately, in elementary school you were never taught how the body communicates to you above and beyond the basics of thirst, hunger and fatigue. And so many of us were raised ignorant of exactly how the body really communicates what it actually needs. Too many of the body's needs are ignored, which is why we become unhealthy. Until now!

Your thoughts have an immediate impact on your body. In a split second, you know whether your way of being and your corresponding thoughts are making you feel good or bad. If you feel good, you know your thoughts and way of being are conducive to your long-term survival. If you feel bad, you know that if you pursue this line of thought, you will do your body—and life—harm.

When we go back to considering time, it is important to receive instant recognition of a thought's consequences. It is essential for long-term survival to know whether who you are being is on the way to enriching you or killing you. Interacting with the environment rarely gives you such an immediate result; manifestation in the physical Universe appears to take time. It is therefore challenging to gain this immediate insight, immediate recognition, without the body as your feedback mechanism. Now all we need to do is become more sensitive to receiving this feedback for optimum life enrichment.

For some, this is liberating. For many others it will mean the end of being irresponsible. It can mean the beginning of being powerfully responsible for the experiences being had here in this lifetime.

Let us take, for example, the times you have felt and had thoughts of love, either for yourself or for others. This feels amazing, doesn't it? Being in a state of love and thinking loving thoughts is a very healing and healthy experience. It is the highest vibrational frequency in the Universe.

> *Your body will always reward you*
> *for loving yourself and others. It is how*
> *it encourages this way of being.*

Likewise, when you have thoughts of jealousy or anger toward another, wanting to hurt another, your body reacts immediately. You may feel satisfied and just, but you will not feel fulfilled, nourished or energized by such thoughts. In fact, such thoughts cripple the body's immune system, leaving you susceptible to all manner of illness.

Consider that every illness, every cut, bruise, burn or stubbed toe, all the way to cancer, are all a result of your way of being. It is how your body, your reality, is communicating the impact your thoughts have on your world!

Too simple? Too obvious? "Surely someone would have discovered this, if it were this simple. If it were really true, I would have heard about it," I hear you say. Once again, another false belief system makes its appearance. For most people, knowing that a happy thought feels good, or a bad thought feels bad, is common sense. For most this is common knowledge.

Treat yourself with love and praise

But what happens to the body when a certain frequency of thought is repeated over and over again —or worse, carried over many years? How does the body respond? How does it talk to you?

What happens when you constantly think the same thoughts of illness, hate, poverty, pain, hardship, victimization, anger, aggression, or of hurting another.

Many of you reading this book have been on this planet long enough to have repeated some of these thoughts several times, several hundred times, or even several thousand times—over and over again. Many of you know it even at a conscious level.

But then there are those who may be thinking: "I don't repeat negative thoughts over and over again, or I don't carry my thoughts and feelings over long periods of time, surely I'd know about it if I did!"

And you would know about it if those thoughts and feelings were occurring in your Conscious Mind. But the thoughts that do the most damage lay somewhere else ... That's right, they reside in your Subconscious Mind, where you store all your beliefs about yourself and your life, hidden from view, but causing even greater damage as they have become part of your physiology.

Is it actually that hard to understand when you think about it, that short-term fears and anxieties cause short-term symptoms like headaches, increased heart rate, and so on, while long-term emotions and beliefs cause long-term symptoms? Who missed this? It is absurd to see illness and disease as separate to the thoughts, feelings and emotions pumping through your body. This would be the same as saying that happy thoughts, such as thoughts of love, happiness and excitement, have no bearing on how well you feel.

The more you have a particular thought, the more this thought grows into what is called a thought form, like a snowball gathering more snow as it rolls down a hill. Consider that within your body, over the years, you have created many different thought forms of hate, anger, resentment, and so on. Thought forms are essentially living energies. They have their own frequency, their own energy mass and momentum. These thought forms, masses of accumulated energies, are stored throughout your body. They are interacting on a daily basis with your organs, your brain, your bones and even your skin. The denser these thought forms, the greater the impact they have on your physical body.

These thought forms interrupt the functioning and healing process, affecting your health and well-being. Otherwise stated, they stop your Soul or True Self from reaching and healing all parts of your anatomy, just like the sun being blocked from warming the earth by clouds.

Intense thought forms of negativity can create all kinds of symptoms in the body, from a common cold to cancer. Different thought forms are stored in different parts of the body. This is essentially how the body communicates to your awareness what specifically is going wrong.

Short-term thoughts or feelings create short-term symptoms, whereas our long-term beliefs, our recurring thoughts, create painful or long-term symptoms. Each part of the body symbolizes a different state of being and its corresponding thoughts. Each organ, muscle and bone represents a way of being, or a thought about an experience.

So to indulge in any thoughts and ways of being that are in any way negative, slowly erodes the natural and perfect functioning of that part of your body. It is easy to understand the body's language by looking at what part of your anatomy or physiology is showing symptoms, or signs of distress or unease.

The body will always start with a whisper, alerting you to a danger ahead. If this signal is heard and appropriate changes are made, no more will be felt on this topic. If, however, you choose to ignore, resist or deny these alarm bells, then the body, for the sake of its survival, has no choice but to speak to you in more dramatic symptoms. The language is all relative to the danger the body is facing.

Healthy Mind = Healthy Body

Healing can only occur when that thought form stops being reinforced by like thought, and when new perspectives—healthy perspectives—are achieved. See life anew and your body will reflect your new perspectives.

What Is The Language Of The Body?

This will give you the basic map on how the body reacts to various states of being. By becoming very clear on this, you will start to develop a much greater relationship and partnership with your body. When a symptom arises, rather than condemning the already wounded body, you will begin to look at how you have been being and therefore how you have been responsible. It is just a feedback loop. Your body will glow when this process begins, as it is the only way to truly look after yourself and to stay on the path to health.

Body Part	Way Of Being
Hair	My sense of self, insecurity and how I feel others perceive me.
Face	Am I OK in this world? Am I showing my best side?
Nose	Am I staying true to my direction?
Ears	Am I listening to my truth?
Eyes Left	How do I see my past?

Look at the stars in wonder

Eyes Right	Am I excited about my future?
Jaw	Am I chewing over decisions? Am I making the right decision?
Neck	Am I agile to roll with the punches, to be flexible and open? How stubborn am I?
Shoulders	Am I being burdened by a sense of responsibility to others?
Arms	Am I being ineffective in grabbing hold of what I need? What's important to me right now?
Hands, Right	Do I have the ability to give generously without fear or regret?
Hands, Left	Do I have the ability to receive graciously without guilt?
Heart	Am I putting pressure on myself to be more or to achieve more? Am I following my path? Am I giving myself self-love?
Lungs	Do I have the ability to allow in more of life?

All Knowing is not separate from you, but part of you

Liver	Am I experiencing anger, resentment and flushing out the toxins from my life experience? Do I carry around anger?
Stomach	Am I hungry for life? How am I digesting the world around me? What am I still holding on to?
Gall Bladder	Do I have disdain for myself or for others?
Kidneys	Do I have balance and equilibrium in my life? Have I allowed toxic experiences in?
Reproductive Organs, Male	Am I creative, bringing ideas to the world? Is my masculinity being allowed to shine?
Reproductive Organs, Female	Do I have the ability to produce and sustain life?
Spine	How much support do I feel I have in my life experience?
Coccyx	Do I need to get moving, wake up, or get off my butt?
Hips	How am I moving forward? Are there perceived obstructions in my path? Where am I being stopped?

Knees	Am I flexible in relationships with others?
Ankles	Am I standing strong and steady in my decisions?
Feet	Am I content in my position in life? Do I love or hate my life right now?

It is not important to memorize these. As you nurture your space of All Knowing, you become proficient in perceiving the thoughts held within your body parts and how best to release them. Follow the Secret Pages to point you in the direction you need to head.

The deeper the thought, the longer you have held onto it, the more it affects your body. Many ill people have the appearance of a balanced state of mind. Do not confuse them with healthy people. It is common that the most damaging of thoughts reside under the surface, hidden from public view. In truth, it is the unconscious beliefs, opinions, or generally held views that cause the most damage... for when a thought, feeling or emotion is raised up to be seen by the Conscious Mind, it can be dissipated immediately. It is your deepest beliefs, thoughts and opinions that you must seek to recognize, those that you may not even know to look for.

It is who we believe ourselves to be, how we perceive our life situation, how we have been treated as both children and adults that lie at the root cause of aging and illness.

Your thoughts at the Subconscious level—the thoughts you have almost no conscious awareness of—and the beliefs about yourself and your life (the ones you would prefer to bury deep down inside) are the most damaging to a human being. They do not just cause illness, but it is our Subconscious beliefs that are our biggest cause of aging.

Beliefs are everything! They show up in our reality, but most importantly they show up in our body first. It is our body's way of bringing up the Unconscious to the Conscious Mind, as a means of keeping us healthy and moving forward. Compare this process to food poisoning, where your body instantly wants to take what is within and exit it out of your system via throwing it up. Illness is simply the body attempting to bring our awareness to thoughts and beliefs that are toxic, in order to exit them from our system also. Now imagine what effect the societal belief "There is no cure for cancer or other illnesses" has on the body's healing process. Belief really is the answer!

How many times do you hear yourself complaining about something, holding on to anger or resentment?

The only one it ultimately hurts is you.

Be grateful for the world you live in

What Is The Root Cause Of Illness?

As Seen Through Whole Brain Intelligence—All Knowing

In a Whole Brain State, I have seen the following as the main causes and solutions to these symptoms:

Illness/Disease	Cause And Cure
Breast Cancer: I am discontent at my ability to bring a life into this world; I am discontent with how I have been toward the people who brought me into this world	To see clearly your Life Purpose and how you count toward the bigger picture, regardless of this belief. Let go of the guilt and move on to bigger things
Cancer (in general): I have a lack of clarity around an event in life, causing much pain and anguish	To see this event with correct perspective, allowing the truth to restore your clarity. It is necessary to forgive the process of life for making this your experience of life

Prostate Cancer:
I am unable to insist that my words are heard and my needs are met in the face of those close to me who oppose me (these people are often disguised as supporters rather than opposers)

To regain your authenticity and power over your life situation; to be a man again

Migraines:
I hate myself to the point that I do not believe I have any worth whatsoever, I feel hopeless

To dispel any negative self beliefs, clearing the past mistakes from your conscious awareness and Subconscious belief system. To start nurturing self-love, through self-nurture and acts of self-love. To remove all influences, people, events or experiences that keep you feeling worthless or like a 'nobody'

Multiple Sclerosis:
I have an inability to love myself because of a fatal flaw— self-disdain

To acknowledge this flaw as a by-product of a greater purpose. Instead, adjust expectations to fitting in with this flaw rather than without it. Love it, embrace it, accept it

AIDS/HIV:
I do not belong here in this way, help me leave

This requires serious belief work, adjusting all self-loathing beliefs, as well as feelings of being misplaced into beliefs that support forward momentum into new circumstances

Parkinson's Disease:
My foundations are unstable, help me to ground in what I know to be real

To remove past experience whereby you felt on shaky ground, clearing any beliefs that life in the future will be shaky as well. This can be resolved with one belief shift: I am stable in myself and my world/ reality

The Common Cold: I am run down, I need rest	Sleep!
The Flu: I am susceptible to how others feel about me and my worth. I believe what others believe	Clear any beliefs around needing others' approval and validation. Ensure you walk your own path, rather than following everyone else's views or version of reality
Insomnia: If I rest, my life will become unstuck	Realign yourself with your life purpose, so that your time is spent wisely, rather than wasted on unproductive activities
Back Ache: Lower Back: I am without the necessary support I believe I require, in order to survive **Upper Back:** Guilt that I have wellbeing and those around me suffer. I am not worthy of my freedom.	Reconnect with the truth, so as to distinguish between what is holding you back and what thoughts set you free. The situation is not as it appears or feels.

Send loving thoughts to those you love, it helps them to heal

Diabetes:
I am undeserving of the pleasures of life/without such pleasures I become a better person. Without my suffering, people are lost.

Realize that past sufferings do not need to be your suffering now. Release the past, knowing your suffering does not aid anyone.

Heart Disease:
I am my own worst enemy. I undermine myself at every turn. I turn away the opportunity to be happy, I am without self love

Clear the limiting beliefs that you have failed yourself and your life. It is time to reconnect with the real you once again.

Obesity In Men:
I am not loved anyway, nobody pays attention to me, I am not acknowledged for who I am

Clear limiting beliefs to clear the need for outward approval, learning to love yourself from within.

Your family is not your anchor; see them as a springboard to greater adventures

Obesity In Women:
I must protect myself from sexual attack, I hate my body, I must shield myself from abuse, I am not letting anyone in/near me

Clear past negative experiences that had you feel unsafe around others, especially men. As above, learn to love yourself independently of others' judgment and insecurities

---

Smoking:
I am not good enough, I do not matter anyway, who cares if I live or die

Getting clarity around how those beliefs were actually formed in error, then shifting those beliefs of self-hate to those of self-belief

---

Again, use this as a guide, but learn to listen to your own body specifically. The Secret Pages teach you how to do that—a skill every human being can benefit from.

The reason this information has not made it into mainstream understanding is exactly because it is so simple. The human body is simple. When it needs something, it tells us. Babies do it from the moment they are born! Why would this innate survival function suddenly change as we mature?

It just gets stronger!

Are There Dual Realities Within Us, Like Split Personalities?

Unbeknown to many, your Consciousness is derived from two main sources. One is fed by your belief system—the Ego; and the other is fed by Universal Intelligence—your Soul, or True Self. It is our Ego that we have been most consumed by in modern times.

> *The True Self is actually the 'brains' behind the operation, while the Ego creates a polar opposite reality, an alternate perspective to live life through.*

The trouble is, these two 'personas' are being used upside-down. The True Self represents unlimited Consciousness, All Knowing harnessed in human form. Your Ego would have you believe it does not exist, but once again this is the opposite of the truth.

The idea is to learn to distinguish who is currently the driver in your life, who are you allowing to make all those important decisions? It is imperative to let in your True Self intelligence, your intuition, to navigate your life instead of your Ego. One creates health and well-being, the other takes it away.

Your Ego attempts to control you through 'small talk'— talk that keeps you small, telling you what cannot be done, or sending you on a wild goose chase, aiming for goals and accomplishments that leave you unfulfilled and unhappy.

Your Ego shouts, your True Self whispers, so you must learn how to still your mind so that your True Self can be heard over the Ego chatter. It is the subtle, soft whispers that need to be followed.

People on Earth have struggled unnecessarily, because many believe they are their opposites (the Ego). In this space they have nothing, so the fear of loss is great. To know oneself as the Universe through the True Self is to know oneself as everyone and everything. You are not without, but full to the brim, needing nothing extra.

The Ego is responsible for the divide between spirituality and science. Without the Ego inverting perception, scientists would see the interconnection between themselves and the spiritual realm as, ironically, the very source of answers they desperately seek.

Have you ever wondered why a coincidence, omen, or synchronicity happens? It is how your True Self communicates when you do not listen directly!

Reconnect with nature by walking, swimming and planting trees

What Is The Relationship Between The True Self And The Body?

Your body is intrinsically related to the intentions of your True Self. They have a purpose for you, a role to play in this movie that is life. Each time your belief systems have you veer away from this role, this path, your body will let you hear about it.

Consider your brain was designed to perceive your True Self, having it be your source of intelligence.

When you let go of needing to be the one who gets to be right, you will access pure genius.

Get out of the driver's seat and hand it over to your chauffeur—your True Self. It is a much more enjoyable ride that way.

The body plays a dual role for the True Self:

1. To provide a physical reality in which to experience life; and

2. To provide a feedback mechanism to the conscious awareness as to the True Self's intentions.

For those not yet directly communicating with their True Self, or not trusting in their intuition as yet, symptoms in the body are the fastest ways for the True Self to communicate to you. Illness and disease are then ways to remind you where you are off track in either

110

your beliefs, decisions or immediate actions.

When this occurs, your True Self has no choice but to remind you that a better path—a higher purpose—has been chosen for this lifetime. This better path is one rich in blessings, filled with happiness, satisfaction and fulfilment, an enlightened experience of life.

To veer away from this path is met with reminders. The early stage of being off track is met with gentle, soft reminders, like a little nudge here and there. For example, to be in fear about one's future (which is not the beingness of a True Self) may be met with shortness of breath, or mild panic attacks. You can call these 'feather reminders,' for they are as light as a feather. Sustained fear of one's future might lead to other, more severe reminders, such as insistent migraines.

This is heading toward what you might call 'brick reminders,' for they hit you a little harder. The longer an unproductive path is pursued, the more severe the alarm bells. Prolonged stubbornness will often result in illness or worse.

These are what you may call being 'hit by a truck,' as they hit hardest and can have you in hospital.

Your True Self and your body play the role of an internal navigation system.

Your True Self as All Knowing can easily survey the landscape, identifying the best possible route for you to take and the best possible decisions to make.

Stubbornness to listen leads to struggle and then illness. Humanity's most debilitating illnesses are caused by prolonged stubbornness—that is to listen to the Ego rather than the True Self.

Persisting along a path not chosen by your True Self will always cause pain and ultimately premature death. Your body cannot survive being off track for prolonged periods of time. It cannot sustain disconnection from its True Self.

To ignore the existence of the True Self is to ignore the very source of life. How can we expect to master the human anatomy when its very essence is overlooked by many of those trying to heal it.

Imagine your body as being the earth and your True Self being the sun. Your beliefs and Ego can be represented as the moon. When the moon eclipses the sun's life-giving rays from reaching the earth for prolonged periods of time, those parts of Earth will begin to decay and die, as do we when we allow our beliefs to block out what is true—our True Self, our Sun.

And so the reminders are there to keep you on track, steering you toward the best possible experience of life. Avoiding illness, pain and suffering is well within everybody's grasp. It does, however, require a shift in beliefs and learning to 'tune in' to one's True Self.

Why have more than one goal in your life when there is just one goal that matters? This goal is to BE your True Self! What other goal brings all others into being? Just one accomplishment will bring all areas of life into balance!

In truth, it is more accurate to say the body reflects how much the True Self is allowed into the body!

Disease and illness are those parts of the body where truth is no longer present, where there is no Soul presence.

SOUL = TRUTH = What Heals!

I am my healer

I am my healer, only I can choose change,
All others can do is light my path.
At the end of the day it's all a farce
If all I do is give up too fast.
My beingness creates my path,
I choose for me what lights my heart.
It's up to me how hard I try,
Because only I know the reason why.
My heart tells me what's true,
I'm lying if I listen to you.
Seek the knowing within my Soul,

Do not anger, do not hate—it solves nothing

And I'll get to see: I am whole.
I can heal my own body,
It's my thoughts that give life,
Not prescriptions, not outside advice.

What is The Solution?

Disease and illness can be healed, but it takes identifying the root cause—or the thought—behind the symptoms to heal them.

The impossible always becomes possible when you have the solution. But the impossible can only become achievable when you accept that it was always possible.

The truth is, there is a cure for cancer—for all cancers —and it is staring us in the face! But we will not find it if we do not know where to look. Look past the body at the thoughts in the mind—there you will see the truth, not the illness.

> *When you identify the root cause of an*
> *experience, physical or otherwise, you set*
> *yourself free to move to another.*

How?

> *The human brain is the most advanced*
> *diagnostic computer ever created!*

Through accessing Whole Brain Intelligence we can perceive the very thoughts (within ourselves or others) that create pain, illness and disease. It is very similar to connecting a cable into the body's computer to ask it exactly why it is under duress. Our brain is just like an X-ray in a way. To help others, Whole Brain Intelligence allows you to redirect your brain to perceive someone else's thought frequencies—in this case the root cause of the illness.

We have seen mechanics plug their diagnostic tools into a car's computer to get a read-out. Well, now you know what we are all capable of doing, metaphorically speaking (without needing a cable!).

Our brain has been designed to perceive thought frequencies. The trick is to re-route it to pick up on those thoughts not belonging to you!

Aging comes from sustaining long periods of disconnection from your True Self. Strengthening the Mind-Body-Soul connection rejuvenates the body.

Learn to access the truth through Whole Brain Intelligence to heal the body.

Is Our Understanding Of God True And Accurate?

The current understanding, the picture so far, is an inaccurate depiction inverted by the mind (Ego) to render human beings powerless over their own life. It is true a pervasive intelligence exists (in fact, layers upon layers of intelligence exist), but it is an All Knowing that is not excluding of anything. It is whole, balanced, and just in every way.

A separate god is an illusion which has been created to maintain particular belief systems. It does not exist. Rather, it is this very intelligence that knows itself as each one of you, as the land, the sea, the stars, the planets; as life perpetuating throughout the Universe. It is pure Consciousness; a concept that many years ago was once manipulated by the human Ego into serving a particular purpose.

Consciousness—a current or field of knowing intelligence—is the basic building block for everything. It is not one thing, but everything. You can talk to this intelligence and perceive insight and wisdom from it. It is not reserved for the characters in history. Rather, it is your innate wisdom, the source of answers that lie within. This 'god' energy is nature, the evolving intelligence pushing new boundaries, expanding and knowing itself anew. If we stop seeing it as separate from ourselves, we will soon start behaving in a far more god-like manner.

*It wants you all to know: "I am you, you are me,
you are one—Consciousness having a big party."*

Decide to see yourself as one with this energy and all the
secrets of the Universe will be yours to play with. Here,
the mysteries are unravelled. Everything is intelligence!

*I have noticed how quick people are to blame
God for natural disasters. Consider we are
ourselves responsible for the shape this planet is
in and the natural shifts occurring worldwide. If
we took responsibility, we could once again create
natural equilibrium for generations to come. The
earth reflects our collective thoughts, just as our
bodies reflect our individual thoughts.*

A Conscious Thinker

As thought and as a thinker, you have profound impact
on your body every minute of every day. We have seen
your thoughts either create health and vitality, a great
life experience; or disease, lethargy and a disappointing
life experience. Yes, you are the creator of your health
and often of your physical death as well.

Your body is your immediate environment. It is the
closest thing to you. As such, it is the most direct access
to feeling who you are being in every moment. Your
role here is to grow and expand, to see yourself as more.

Resentment only hurts you

Put the other way around, you will also reflect how big or small you see yourself. Everything, after all, is just a mirror reflection.

What does this all mean to you? It means to start or continue to be very conscious of your thoughts.

> *The more conscious you are, the less damage you do to yourself and others; and the greater and more fulfilling your life becomes.*

People may believe that you have little or no control over thoughts. They just pop in and pop out. This is true to a degree; however, you can exert control over your state of being. It is your state of being that dictates the type or vibration of thoughts you think. How you are being attracts certain thoughts.

Therefore, it is very important to be mindful at all times of how you are being. Powerful beingness creates powerful thoughts. Powerful thoughts create powerful decisions and powerful decisions create powerful outcomes.

Some examples of states of being include: powerful, miserable, depressed, vengeful, resentful, jealous, aggressive, arrogant, loving, joyous, inspiring, peaceful, generous ...

It is important to spend a few moments discussing the importance of being, as it extends beyond physical well-being. Beingness is a creative or destructive thought pattern. It interacts with your physical environment, as it directs specifically charged thoughts. But how you are being is what actually gives a thought its emotional charge. Without a decent emotional charge, a thought has little ability to amass enough energy to materialize or manifest. How you are being is the secret ingredient to creating everything your True Self desires.

If you look honestly, you will already see a perfect correlation between who you are being and the life you are living. When you are being loving, you do not only feel love pumping through your entire being, but you also create love and loving relationships around you. When you are being courageous, you feel strong, invincible, and able to conquer previously insurmountable obstacles. People feel your courage and you find yourself getting what you want a lot more frequently and quickly.

Likewise, when you are being aggressive, angry, vengeful, jealous or vindictive, you pollute your energy and body with a very low frequency of energy. This type of energy is poisonous to your body. Your body is naturally of a high vibration. Therefore, to inject it with negativity reduces your health and lifespan.

Being this way will also attract similar people and situations to your life. Your body has a natural resonance that matches your True Self. Thinking thoughts incongruent with this resonant frequency affects your health and well-being.

The most productive forms of
Beingness come from your True Self—
these can be found in a space of stillness.

All is revealed within the Secret Pages.

My Reflections

Why Did The Concept Of 'Thought' Present Itself In Our Lives?

It has been a long-standing notion that everything within our Universe is, at its essence, 'Energy.'

But to me this theory was insufficient. It did not explain Consciousness, Self-Awareness, the intelligence behind the design of our species, the purposefulness behind the animal kingdom and the superior intelligence exhibited throughout nature. It certainly did not explain an apparent subtle guiding force causing us all to learn particular lessons in life, among other things.

So, one day, I sat quietly with my All Knowing Self and asked, "What are we missing in our understanding of the very nature of the Universe?"

It was then that I was shown that everything begins with a thought; that nothing is separate from thought; that the Universe is more than energy—so much more! The Universe is intelligent energy, particles of self-awareness binding together to create like-minded entities, made purely of thought. The Universe is made entirely of this thought substance, being self-aware and exploring itself in many different ways.

Truth 3

Stillness

"Stillness Unlocks The Door To The
True Self. A Busy Mind Closes It."

Be in awe of the human form

What is Stillness?

Those who have had the experience of stillness know that this is the absence of thought. It is simply just being.

Peace and stillness dramatically affect the quality of our experience of being alive. It affords us great insight into our world and on how best to evolve and grow in our own lives. Our growth and evolution inevitably leads to greater happiness in our lives; this is what makes stillness a most worthwhile pursuit.

Stillness is that space where all answers can be found. It is a state of consciousness that links the Conscious Mind to the Subconscious, the Subconscious to the True Self, and beyond—All Knowing.

Stillness enables you access to a Whole Brain State of Consciousness. This means you begin to utilize a far greater brain capacity than you ever believed possible.

A Whole Brain State of Consciousness grants you abilities others would deem as super-sensory or highly intuitive. New information is gleaned in just seconds through intuition, without needing to even think about it.

This Whole Brain State is far more nurturing than a mind filled with the clutter and noise of thought. It heals and rejuvenates the body into perfect balance.

Stillness allows far more into your life. It is the one true source of perfect living, as from this space you can create—in every sense of the word.

How Do We Cultivate Stillness?

Stillness is simply the absence of the mind and its constant, random, busy thoughts—eliminating the distraction of one's Ego.

Stillness is created by being Ego free.
The less you believe the thoughts stemming from your Ego, the less mind chatter you experience.

Ironically, it is only in stillness that your True Self can be accessed. The Ego is clutter and noise, the True Self comes in stillness and peace. Once again, the opposite plays out in our life—so we must turn it upside down.

Stillness is the beginning of realizing the unimaginable potential that lies deep within. Only in stillness can you access All Knowing.

Stillness allows you to bypass the
influences of your belief system.

Fortunately, there are many ways to move from an active mind to a place of stillness. Removing one's Ego (see Secret Pages) is the fastest access to stillness.

In addition, a way to cement stillness in the mind is to practice or cultivate stillness in life. We habitually make our lives full and hectic to avoid seeing ourselves. Being busy is often just avoidance, preventing you from stopping and seeing how you really feel about things.

Ultimately, the slower you move through life, the greater your ability to create stillness. The next time you do anything, watch the speed at which you do it.

Watch how we so often reduce our tasks and experiences to just a means to an end, hoping that someday soon our 'real life' will happen. And then we will be grateful, appreciative, and stop to smell the roses. The next time you find yourself doing something, ask yourself, "Am I even present to life right now, or is it a means to an end?" The slower your thoughts, the greater your self-awareness becomes. This aids you in creating the states of being that best support your endeavors.

Until you can slow down enough to develop this self-awareness, it can be more challenging to control your states of being, let alone deliberately choose a state of being for the moment, the day, or your life.

Any state of being creates—it creates consistent thoughts and it creates your material world around you. So how, then, do you create how you are being? How do you choose which space you need to be in and how do you hold it?

A way of being that is directed—or preferred—comes from total presence, and this comes from being Ego free. The more self-aware you are in every moment, the more power you have to determine and alter your state of being. Each state of being creates a different outcome in life. Angry states of being create experiences that will make you or others angry. Enlightened states of being create enlightened experiences for you and others.

124

You may have noticed that those who lack self-awareness are constantly in and out of unproductive states of being, otherwise known as mood swings, or moody personalities. In such situations, their lack of self-awareness leaves them victim to default and reactionary ways of being, sourced from their beliefs (Ego). These usually appear as jealousy, anger, frustration, vengefulness, and aggression.

Those who live with high self-awareness will tend to oscillate between very few states of being, as they keep choosing the states that are the most productive and the ones that feel the best and are safest for the body. They are also the states of being that create the best decision-making.

To move slowly through your day, being present in every moment, reconnects you with your body and its sensations. Smells, tastes and sensations become more vibrant, emotions more satisfying, and your ways of being become more resilient to fragmenting influences.

Next time you eat a meal, turn the TV off. The next time you drive your car, drive without the radio on. The next time you talk to a loved one on the phone, do not do anything else in that moment. The next time you take a walk, walk slower—much slower. Slow down, do not pack your days too full, focus on one thing at a time and be present in the moment without allowing your thoughts to go elsewhere. Such a simple practice and you will regain your life, one that is worth living.

Cherish every minute you spend with loved ones

Stillness creates self-awareness and vice versa, both are disciplines that we all need to cultivate, no matter what level we are at. Stillness affords us great insight over our life: what food to eat, how best to talk to one another to get the best outcome, and how best to allow in our intuition. In greater states of self-awareness, a Whole Brain State of intelligence can be accessed, where your brain becomes more finely tuned to the subtler thoughts that lay underneath your conscious awareness. This is the beginning of Accessing All Knowing.

It's amazing how much more you can get done when you move much more slowly—in stillness. Once again, the Ego has tricked us into thinking speed, rather than stillness, equals productivity.

My Reflections

What about Meditation?

So many people are under the impression that meditation holds the key. I pondered this, wondering if this was the case. Why are there so many people who meditate, but are still without answers? The answer I received was: Meditation is one access to stillness in the mind. Stillness in the mind removes the Ego and it is in an Ego-free zone where All Knowing is accessed.

So, in truth, the real purpose behind meditation is not stillness for stillness' sake, but rather to go beyond stillness and connect to the answers that lay within.

Truth 4

Two Halves Make A Whole

"The Human Brain, Misunderstood By So Many, Actually Transcends Space And Time. It Knows Only The Boundaries We Impose On It, Limiting It To The Here And Now."

Whole Brain Intelligence

Your brain does more than you know.
It's not stand-alone, as you've been told.
It perceives frequencies just like a radio.
The more still your mind is, the more you will know.
Your brain has two halves that make it whole.
To utilize one is to go without Soul.
Your whole brain works as one,
Allowing you to 'tune in' and have some fun.
Like an antenna in your head,
Your brain can see all, before it is said.
You've all allowed this intelligence in,
It happens only when your thoughts are thin.
Genius knocks at your door,
When you engage your Whole Brain, nothing more.
You've experienced this all before
When you've felt someone's thoughts at your door.
You've felt your loved one's fear,
Though they weren't even near.
You've felt a 'vibe' in a room,
As if someone was surely doomed.
You see fish swim in unison, birds flock effortlessly,
Why can't you see, you belong to a harmony.
To wake at 3 a.m. with inspiration on its way,
Is not something random to just throw away.
Instead, it's time you listen—it's urgent;
Begin using your brain to its fullest purpose.
You have shut down your mind with anger and doubt,
Which limits you to go without.
Your beliefs about life steer you so wrong,

Leading you down the proverbial song.
Beliefs dictate and your brain will act,
See more for yourself and you'll end the lack.
Genius is not born just from the brain;
It's a state of being, that's not insane.
The more self-belief you carry within,
The more your brain can allow in.
To trash yourself, your life and your planet,
Is the equivalent of hitting your brain with a mallet.
As a radio, your brain broadcasts your thoughts,
Your brain perceives All Knowing, picking up from naught.
Your brain can see for miles into space,
Accessing information on every place.
True creativity, wisdom without bounds,
Unlimited knowledge is yours to be found.
All Knowing is available to all life forms;
Without it, life wouldn't be born.
Your environment needs you to evolve,
There are endless possibilities to be told.
Peace within is a stone's throw away,
When you read this book and don't throw it away.
An All Knowing Brain sees all,
Never trashes anything at all.
It holds all the answers to all your questions,
You are not alone as many have mentioned.
Explore the truth within these pages,
To allow yourself to live for ages.
On this journey you will find
The secret keys to unlock your mind!

Avoid drugs and chemicals in your system

How Do We Best Harness The Human Brain?

To date, the vast majority of human beings have used the brain to solve their problems and answer their questions. In fact, the human brain has been used for just about everything it should not be used for.

Confused?

Look around you, witness the destructive impact of mankind and then look at nature and begin to amaze at the beauty, perfection and equilibrium that is your Universe. Nowhere will you see the same destructive prowess in the natural world as in the world created by ideas coming from the human brain.

Clearly something is missing.

Your brain's main purpose is to provide you awareness over the ecosystems that you belong to; to source new information instead of regurgitating old data; to function our body harmoniously instead of applying demands on it.

All life is intelligent. Life cannot exist without intelligence! This is so clearly evident when you see the harm decisions without intelligence have done to people, the planet and its inhabitants.

What does 'to source information' mean? Isn't the brain designed to think?

What if, instead of using our brain to problem-solve, we

use it to access the intelligence displayed everywhere within nature? What if we, too, could utilize the very same 'mind' that has the world rotate from night to day, season to season? What if we, too, could access the brilliance that carved the world we see before us?

By now you know, we actually can!

Nature is your Nature!

Achieving a Whole Brain State of Consciousness affords us the ability to draw on the intelligence we see throughout our natural world. We call this intelligence— this 'mind'—Ui (Universal Intelligence), or All Knowing.

> *The brain was built to draw on the collective wisdom, knowledge and genius that surround us—Universal Intelligence, All Knowing. It is available for all living things to draw on for their sustenance, survival, or for the betterment of their lives.*

Our minds can draw on this field of energy for knowledge, wisdom and answers.

People's intuition draws on this field continuously, but the lay persons using only their stand-alone brain power are too trapped in their busy thoughts to recognize its presence or to harness its full genius.

Intuition is simply a heightened awareness to perceive thought frequencies or energy frequencies outside the brain, which a Whole Brain State provides. It is nothing scary, freaky or strange. It is totally natural within every human being, except that in the Western world we have not used it in our everyday lives for a long time—and as we all know, what you do not use, you lose. So we must re-learn what we have forgotten.

Three levels of Consciousness:
the Subconscious is your current reality, the True
Self is your unlimited reality, and the Conscious
Mind chooses which one to believe.

Your personal link to All Knowing is your True Self.

The True Self funnels in the necessary energy or information you need to grow and evolve through your brain for your understanding. Much of the information you need is encoded into your DNA as a means of keeping you on track as soon as you are born. Intuition comes from both your DNA and your True Self. Your brain is certainly capable of drawing information from other than these sources, yet these sources are personalized to you.

Your True Self, once you are connected, governs which information you draw upon to ensure your behaviors are ecological, as seen in nature. When connected beyond your brain, you cannot help but be ecological; it is the very essence of All Knowing.

Humanity is on the brink of expansion.
We all have to choose between what others
are telling us we want versus that which
our heart is telling us we need.

Your brain is designed to draw on this information and bring it to you in a way you can understand. This is how you can access eighty to one hundred percent of your brain, rather than using a mere three to five percent of it, as most people do now.

Try to understand that the Universe has been based on efficiency, on getting the right information to the right places with ease. Here is where your brain comes in ... you are part of the electrical field that is the Universe—a current of energy that sustains all life and is the source of your All Knowing.

This field can also be described as Nature, as the Ecosystem—a subtly guiding intelligence, allowing all things to flourish and expand simultaneously. Your brain tunes in to the frequencies found in this current as information, just like a radio tunes in to radio frequencies. The more still and quiet your mind is, the greater the number of frequencies you can access, and the more information you can 'download.'

To need to be better than others has you be less—
to be more is to be a better version of yourself, for yourself

Can We Access External Intelligence?

'Downloading,' or accessing external intelligence, requires a special configuration of the brain. We call this configuration a Whole Brain State. Your brain, in a Whole Brain State, becomes just like a radio transmitter, now able to both broadcast frequencies far and wide, and also to receive frequencies from far and wide, a.k.a. Accessing All Knowing.

We have all allowed this information to drift in at various stages in our life, which is why many people wake at 3 a.m. with a flash of genius, or why you can feel someone staring at you. Who has ever felt when your partner is upset or angry at you? We all have!

This is the main purpose of the human brain, to function as a tuner and amplifier of existing intelligence; and that is actually what it does best. As a tuner, the brain decides what information to 'tune in' to, like a radio dial sets the frequency on a radio. As an amplifier, the brain harnesses intelligence and has the body act on that intelligence to fulfil a purpose.

Humanity, in general, utilizes a rather modest percentage of their total brain capacity, drawing on this field of intelligence very rarely. This accounts for the topsy-turvy state of affairs people's lives—and the planet as a whole—are in. Human beings have largely closed

---

Do not succumb to peer group pressure,
the mainstream are in the dark

down their access to this field through stubbornness, negativity, and the general limiting beliefs held in society about ourselves as a species.

"We're only human after all," we say. We are actually superhuman ...All Knowing Consciousness in one awesome package! When we make decisions in our normal operating mode—using our stand-alone brain rather than our Whole Brain Intelligence—we are not receiving the benefit of the collective intelligence that vastly surpasses the here and now and our memories. In stand-alone mode, we often make decisions that are constrained by what we know, based on our limiting beliefs.

Decisions from Whole Brain Intelligence are rejuvenating for your body, congruent with your internal ecosystem, and beneficial to your external ecosystems. In other words, Whole Brain Intelligence—accessing All Knowing—allows all ecosystems to remain in balance, as balance is predicated upon All Knowing, not self-doubt.

Is There A Human Internet?

There exists a library of sublime magnitude, available to us all. It is called Energy. Everything is energy. Energy carries information. Information is therefore everywhere! Your brain perceives energy. Turn on that powerful antenna—your brain—and 'tune in' to information everywhere!

In a Whole Brain State, your brain is limitless in possibility, just like a computer harnessing the internet. Thanks to the internet, a computer's intelligence went from being limited to what was on its hard drive to the intelligence contained on any and every other computer connected to it through the internet.

Whole Brain Intelligence does to your brain what the internet did to the humble computer. After all, where do you suppose the idea for the internet even came from? Once again, we see the micro of the macro!

Can We All Access Genius On Demand

True genius is inspired, meaning it does not come from the brain, but rather through it—you need to be open and allowing to receive genius.

In this opposite world, we spend our time trying and forcing information and genius to surface, as we are taught by the Ego world. Instead, All Knowing is within everyone, simple to access. Keep turning it upside down and you will get to see the whole picture!

Unlimited creativity, enlightened wisdom and infinite knowledge are available to us all through this All Knowing Field. Those flashes of genius that hit when you least expect it are a small sample of what this Field of All Knowing has available. In truth, we can access it on demand. That is how the brain was intended, 24/7-access to pure intelligence. It is available to you— if you choose it.

Your imagination is the gateway to the Universe, it syncs your conscious reality to Consciousness as a whole—the Universe, All Knowing.

Is Imagination The Doorway To Infinity?

The imagination taps the vast recesses of your mind ... or does it? When properly used, your imagination is intended for 'virgin thought,' the product of All Knowing.

The greatest minds throughout history have all had one thing in common—they believed in their imagination. Many people today carry the belief that imagination means 'not real,' or 'fantasy' (another word misused in

---

Do not assume every school is OK for your child

society), and hence they do not access their imagination the way it was intended—to receive intelligence. Understanding the true purpose of your imagination helps you to access your All Knowing. It creates self-belief, one of the major keys to All Knowing.

Your imagination re-awakens Whole Brain Intelligence, allowing you to perceive information beyond what you know in your head.

What Is Intuition? Is It Real or Fake?

By now you are understanding that intuition is far more than a gut reaction, especially as most gut reactions are driven by your Subconscious beliefs rather than an All Knowing within. Your intuition is a very real part of your capabilities, far greater than some give credit. It is All Knowing. Though many think it is fake, ironically it is actually the only real aspect to you. Remember to turn it upside down!

Your intuition is Whole Brain Intelligence. We can use the word intuition and Whole Brain Intelligence interchangeably. It is your inbuilt antenna, just like what ants or bees have on top of their head! In this state, your brain can perceive your entire world beyond what your five physical senses can detect, taking you from using only three to five percent of your brain to using your entire brain capacity.

INTUITION
IS YOUR
INSTRUCTION
MANUAL

***It is your five physical senses
that perceive physical reality. Your
intuition—your sixth sense—perceives
the non-physical reality—all thought!***

Your intuition governs your well-being. It is the missing
link to extraordinary living. Take a moment to remember
the outcomes from ignoring your intuition.

Now remember the outcomes from listening to your
intuition. Which will you choose from now on?

The more you nurture your intuition through believing
and trusting in it, the more intelligence you can access.
Again, stillness is often a major prerequisite, as it can be
difficult to access All Knowing over our loud, cluttered
thoughts.

Your True Self is All Knowing unto itself, but can
also act as a modem to other sources of information,

139

other frequencies. Your True Self is connected to the Universe's world-wide web, All Knowing.

Your brain in a Whole Brain State was designed to access thought frequencies, because that is what your True Self is. Your True Self is pure thought—your Soul. How else is it to run the show if your body and brain cannot hear it? It is your internal guidance system—the source of your intuition. Your beliefs dictate how much of this All Knowing you get to access, how fast you access it, and for what purposes.

Beliefs are the kink in the hosepipe of All Knowing.

The more open we are to allowing in new perspectives and alternate realities, the faster we can evolve!

Why Resist?

A strange phenomenon exists where those confronted by the prospect of greatness begin to fear loss in their lives ... fear of what we stand to give up permeates our thoughts, fear of the sacrifices we will need to endure along this 'enlightened' journey.

The joke is that we have already given up, lost and sacrificed greatly. Seeking more for ourselves is the end of sacrifice! There is no greater sacrifice than the denial of our own greatness. So what is the risk really? It is only up from here!

Which do you choose? Disconnection? The status quo?
A mediocre experience? Or do you choose an alternate
reality, where anything is possible, with unlimited
intelligence at your fingertips?

Is Fate A Choice?

Every day, we face many new choices, decisions that
recreate future paths. Every one of us chooses the life
we experience in every moment of every day. Fate is not
the future, as some might think. Rather, fate is the best
possible path that brings fulfilment. Therefore, fate is
not a future outcome, but a present moment decision
to be made.

So how do you allow in the right decision to fulfil your
destiny when so many people want to have their say—
their way or the highway? It is in stillness, not in anger,
fear or hate, but in calm stillness that we can feel our
way to the right choices.

Your Beingness dictates the thoughts and information
that flood into your mind. Your decisions based on angry
thoughts lead to angry outcomes. Your decisions based
on needing to prove yourself create empty outcomes of
still needing to prove yourself.

Your decisions based from within a calm, centered space
deliver calm, centered outcomes.

Another's truth is not necessarily your own ...
follow your heart, it is where your truth exists

What space are you making all your decisions from?

Hate or love? Anger or peace? Resentment or gratitude? Inadequacy or wholeness? Calm yourself to make only the best decisions from the best possible space. See the Secret Pages for guidance on how to do this.

I Am Not Creative … Or Am I?

Not many realize or understand this, but your imagination has no bounds. The mind is Consciousness and so it connects to Consciousness … and Consciousness is not limited to the physical body or your brain.

> *Your creativity is not limited by your knowledge, skills or ability, but only by your beliefs about yourself.*

The physical Universe is said to be never ending, infinite. This is because that is the nature of Consciousness—it too is limitless, as, therefore, is your imagination.

Your imagination is pure Consciousness, limited only by how you see yourself and your reality. The less limiting or obstructing beliefs you hold, the more of infinity you get to access.

The human mind is made up of sensors that both react and interact with their environment. These sensors, like tiny hairs on your skin, detect virtually imperceptible frequencies of Consciousness, feeding the mind information—your intuition.

Access to All Knowing becomes available when we ignore standard conventions for learning, opening ourselves up to the enormous possibility that what we need, we already have within!

Learning does not need to come just from books or other people, but can also come through the brain. How do you think this book was written? Not by reading other people's books!

This new version of reality, of gaining insights and understanding from outside the brain, gives way to new thought—radically advanced ideas and concepts. This not only creates an entirely new future, but also prevents the same old patterns and habits being repeated over and over again.

The truth is all of us know we have everything we need within, but the Ego acts as a gateway to this knowledge, fencing out what is new and revolutionary.

We have been told we need a degree to be smart, that we need training to perform our function in life. The truth is, we do have everything we need inside. Our brain is a doorway to infinity.

INFORMATION

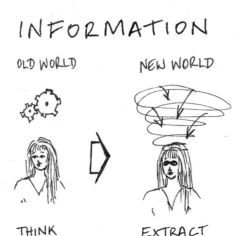

OLD WORLD   NEW WORLD

THINK   EXTRACT

A human being is a highly self-sufficient organism intended and designed that way—we are Consciousness personified.

Giant breakthroughs in all areas—from technology, human anatomy and so on—are available through this type of learning. Some call this 'channeled learning,' but in truth it is no different from inspiration, from accessing genius at random times, in random moments, in a dream, while using the bathroom, or when writing a book.

The difference here is that this Genius, your All Knowing, is accessed on demand. Any concept, any topic, any solution can be gleaned through accessing Whole Brain Intelligence. The truth of the matter is that the brain is simply a filter to the non-physical Universe. The body is the 'experiencer' within the physical Universe. The brain perceives what is present in the energy of thought while the body uses this information to advance its own Consciousness and that of the collective Consciousness.

All Knowing is a state of being unlike any other. It does not require the thinking processes of the brain, but rather mental stillness.

We all have supersensory capabilities. Many of us experience these abilities on a regular basis, but most do not because their beliefs do not allow it. However, true All Knowing comes as a by-product of something special, something unfortunately rare in these times— Self-Belief.

How Can I Tell The Difference Between Intuition & Ego?

All Knowing becomes immediately available in every instance that you connect to your True Self. It is the True Self that is All Knowing by nature. Your much neglected intuition draws on this All Knowing field, helping you stay abreast of possible dangers to your health and your life, as well as opportunities flowing your way.

But how do you know the difference between your beliefs making your decisions versus pure intuition?

Exercise moderately and regularly—avoid extremes

It has been a sad state of affairs, but the rise of the Ego has grown so dramatically that very few can distinguish its impulses from the messages of your intuition—the voice of your True Self.

As unfortunate as it may seem, we must grow to nurture our intuition to become once again the prevalent influence over our feelings and therefore our overall decision-making.

How is this done?

First of all, within the Secret Pages you will find step-by-step instructions on how to clear the influence of your Ego, so keep this tool at the ready. But how do you then ensure it is your intuition speaking rather than your Ego creeping in once again?

The secret is all in your intention. There are those intentions that speak to the Ego, and then there are those intentions that only speak to the True Self. Intentions that speak to your Ego are intentions that come from comparison to others. Intentions that speak to the True Self are questions about becoming more whole and complete within yourself.

To ask the question "How do I get this new job promotion?" brings out more Ego than "How do I best walk my Soul Purpose?"

You see, your mind wants validation, whereas your True Self wants you to experience a sense of wholeness and completion. Two different questions achieve your intention, but only one calls your Ego into being. Questions that relate to your needing to be more in another person's eyes bring out the Ego more than questions that come from wanting to experience who you really are. One comes from lack, one comes from wholeness.

Example: "How do I make more money?"

Rewrite: "What's in my highest good to experience myself as wealthy?"

You also know where you have come from based on how the answers make you feel. An Ego question leaves you feeling stuck in old patterns and thinking.

A True Self-space question leaves you feeling motivated and uplifted. An absence of truth will always leave you feeling conflicted in some way or another. See for yourself, experience and practice being Ego free, so you can see just how different these two spaces are. It will soon become very obvious which space you can rely on.

What Unlocks Whole Brain Intelligence?

This is a topic that in recent times has been highly neglected. While there has been much talk on manifestation, nutrition, and expanded awareness, very few have given this topic the attention it most certainly deserves.

Self-belief is the missing ingredient in nearly every human being's life. Only a tiny few, a handful of human beings, are free of self-doubt in their life.

While many success stories and sporting heroes have
extraordinary self-belief and conviction in one area of
their lives, many of them lack self-belief and therefore
abundance in other areas of their lives.

The high achievers who you see and hear about rarely
excel at more than one thing, more than one area of life.
They may be exceptional and even miraculous at sports,
but dismal failures in money, relationships, business,
parenting, or wisdom.

This example is not to cut these people down. It is
merely to demonstrate when just one area of life is
rich with self-belief. Now imagine a life where self-
belief is prevalent in all aspects, in all areas of life. What
a place this would be if this trait was nurtured and
practiced in the lives of millions—even billions! Even
self-belief being nurtured in just hundreds would cause
a monumental shift in the Consciousness of the planet
and our quality of life.

148

Whole Brain Intelligence—accessing your True Self—occurs when self-belief is present, when the mind is still. In non-self-belief states, we draw on our default operating system instead, designed specifically to run our body, not make decisions.

As a society, we are living predominantly through self-doubt, feeling not enough. As such, we spend the majority of time accessing only a small portion of our brain's true capabilities. In self-belief, both hemispheres of our brain work in unison, able to pick up on our True Self and other sources of intuition, rather than just our own stand-alone intelligence.

Our beliefs have us feel our five physical senses are all there is (it is just not true, we are Consciousness through and through, before we are even human). And so, very few of us have been brought up knowing otherwise. Our brain does as instructed, nothing more. If we presume we have no other intelligence available, then nor does our brain.

So to become limitless—All Knowing—learn to draw on this intelligence as the default setting, rather than stand-alone intelligence. The more you begin to trust in these capabilities, higher intelligence begins to integrate within you, becoming one with your everyday waking awareness. Some call this the process of Enlightenment.

Choose simplicity over complexity, Soul over Ego

Why Self-Belief?

Self-belief is the critical condition that makes Whole Brain Intelligence possible. Without it, the brain disconnects from All Knowing. The truth behind this is that the True Self is pure self-belief—All Knowing. To access the True Self frequency, you must be able to match it with your own frequency of self-belief.

So what actually is self-belief? The irony is that it is not belief. What self-belief is directing your awareness to is the inner knowing of who and what you truly are. You do not need belief when you have knowing. Nothing holds more conviction than true and authentic knowing.

Your True Self is pure knowing. Self-doubt comes from your beliefs—it is your Ego. The Ego is the opposite of your True Self. True Self is self-belief—All Knowing; Ego is self-doubt.

Belief is laced with doubt, waiting to be overcome or merged into knowing. Belief is a good way to begin, prior to accessing your knowing. It is totally OK to have belief; there are times when all you have is belief.

But belief is nowhere near as strong as knowing. Knowing and believing are both states of being. You are either in one or the other, not both. You cannot be in knowing if you are in believing, and you have transcended believing if you are now in knowing.

Don't take life so seriously, find out what
stops you from laughing so much

Where do you spend most of your time? In knowing or believing? Or neither?

What does it mean to truly know something, as opposed to believing in it?

Knowing as a state of being is the difference between cement and sand. To build a house in cement will certainly last a lot longer than building its foundations in sand. To know something is to have no doubt.

Knowing is the experience of feeling, of 'having arrived.' It is the sensation in your body of already being at the finish line before you have even taken your first step.

For years, personal development material has tried to capture this success factor. They have described the process of creative visualization, of cutting out pictures of your goals and sticking them to your refrigerator, or on a vision board. But none have really captured the true essence, the ultimate sensation, of knowing.

Many speak of self-confidence, of feeling deserving and worthy. Some talk about believing in your ability to manifest anything. What all these presentations, books, tapes and CDs are lacking is this essential ingredient— that is, the difference between belief and knowing.

Knowing has an entirely different vibration and resonance than believing. Believing tells the Universe that you feel confident it can happen. Knowing tells the Universe that it is already happening and to make it a reality in time and space.

Knowing tells the body that you are healthy, abundant, and in control. Believing tells the body that you are an optimist, someone that believes you deserve great things to happen to you, someday, somewhere.

How Do We Live In Knowing?

So, how do you go from mistrusting to self-belief and then to knowing? In one sense, it is what your entire life process is about, but that is the long way home. You can move into knowing without living out the entirety of your physical life. It is not easy, but it sure is simple. Do not expect this to be an overnight process, it will take discipline and maybe some strange looks from family and friends, but the joys at the finish line and the breakthroughs along the way are a true gift—one of the best things life has to offer.

Are you ready to learn more? Yes, of course!

It is your beliefs that prevent knowing, specifically the beliefs that say I'm not enough. It is also beliefs or thoughts that create prerequisites to knowing. To believe you need something prior to knowing is the first step in the opposite direction away from knowing.

Knowing is like all other ways of being. It is simply that—a way of being. Like most states of being, populations of people believe in the compulsory necessity of prerequisites:

∞   To be happy, I must first pay off all my bills.

∞   To feel loved, I must have a life partner or family.

∞ To be successful, I must be rich or famous.

Humans are very well practiced in this paradigm. This is a paradigm you might recognise as: HAVE before I can DO, before I can BE (e.g. HAVE a lot of money, so I can DO what I want, so I can BE happy).

As discussed earlier, in a space of stillness one gets to choose their way of being ... and ways of being create reality. So, a way of being requires nothing and needs nothing separate from everything you currently are and have.

Being in a state of knowing requires the letting go, the dissolving of a need for prerequisites, conditions, or physical/material possessions.

As long as you believe you need more, you will be right.

Knowing comes after believing. It is vastly greater than confidence, as it is derived from something larger than yourself. Knowing is an innate condition stemming from perceiving the non-physical realm you are part of. It is a level of awareness, and in this space there are no unknowns, speculations, or doubts—there is just knowing. Knowing comes after connecting with your True Self and it is at the point where all your beliefs around self-doubt have been laid to rest.

Knowing is a completely different way to interact on this planet. It requires nothing. Any belief that suggests

---

Death is not the end, just a new beginning

you need something to know is the first obstacle on your path. So be aware of all the beliefs as they pop up for you. Secondly, knowing does not require anyone else, anywhere else, to have proven the viability, plausibility or possibility of what it is you are seeking to experience. This is another misconception that keeps the growth of mankind constrained and small. This way of thinking allows only incremental shifts in thinking and experiencing.

> *Radical breakthroughs, on the other hand, have no prerequisites—they just happen. There is no trying, just allowing them to be received.*

Our beliefs constrain what is possible, just like pushing possibility through a cookie cutter. So, knowing that knowing requires nothing—no prerequisites, no proof—already has you eighty percent on your way to knowing! The next twenty percent of knowing is achieved by the understanding of doubt. Doubt is the opposite of knowing, and it is always present in believing—even if only in fractions, it is nonetheless present.

Doubts are any thoughts and/or emotions that cloud over possibility. They are poison to your garden of creation. You have doubts—you do not invite them, but they are always there. So, how do we arrive at knowing in the face of doubt?

This is the simple, but not easy, part. Doubt is nothing more than a series of fear-based questions. Do I really deserve this? Is this possible? What will people think of

154

me? How will I ever find the money for this? How can I get the time off work? Etc, etc, etc.

This is your way of pre-empting failure and creating contingencies on how you would cope in a failure result. So doubt is fear and fear is just a method of coping with failure.

If fear is the coping with failure, you can see how easy it is to remove the fear, yes? If you remove the possibility of failure, then you have nothing to fear. If you have nothing to fear, then you have no reason to doubt, correct?

And now a paradigm shift awaits you. Fear and knowing actually cancel each other out. Fear and knowing are both based in a world that requires no prerequisites, no past experience and no evidence of either ever having happened anywhere, at any time.

To know, you need no evidence, no prerequisites, and no past evidence. To fear, you need no evidence, no prerequisites, and no past evidence. You can fear having a car crash or a plane crash without having ever experienced it before. You can also experience fear of being a failure at something new without anyone having failed at that in the past. Both knowing and failure are concepts that exist without the need for evidence.

To live in a space of knowing requires the acceptance that anything is in fact possible. The mind needs evidence to see possibility. This is why there are so few enlightened beings on Earth today. The Ego has become so strong that it is rare for a true breakthrough in perception to happen. The concept of evidence is a man-made phenomenon. It has been created by Ego to allow baby steps to be made, rather than quantum shifts. If you can accept that evidence is not required, then you have taken the first step to creating quantum leaps in thinking, and more importantly in creating.

Let us summarize to help you on your path:

The Universe does not need evidence to materialize anything. You prevent that which you want by blocking its creation. You do this repeatedly by needing prerequisites or evidence of possibility. Possibility can only come from pure imagination. Doubt comes from fear of failure. Failure is canceled out by knowing. To no longer need evidence has you free from worrying about failure.

Fear is eliminated when you are one with your Knowing—a typical chicken or the egg concept.

Or is it?

Fear is a by-product of something much deeper. Fear comes from a disconnection, or a disassociation with your True Self. Your True Self is always in a state of Knowing—All Knowing. It never falters and it never fails you. Therefore, the fastest access to a permanent state of knowing and of true empowerment is not through others and their teachings, but through reconnecting with your True Self.

Imagine if all your decisions came from the sum total of All Knowing. This would mean every decision would be based on every event, every decision, and every possible future outcome— that is becoming Limitless! And that is what is available for everyone!

This connection is what made it possible to write this book. It is this connection that will ensure perfect health, maximum longevity, the end of suffering, the end of scarcity and the end of hatred on this planet.

For centuries, mankind has looked to books, looked for idols, false prophets and egotistical leaders for answers and salvation. All this has achieved is billions of disempowered and confused people. You have come with me on this journey so far. You have learned many new things about yourself and the world you live in. Now I am extending you an invitation to the world, an invitation for you to learn how to reconnect with your True Self. If you answer "Yes," you will find the answer contained within this book. If you answer "No," put the book down and I thank you for your company.

It is, however, much easier to navigate your life when being All Knowing than not.

Yes or no? This is a 'choose your own adventure,' just like life. If you choose yes, you will find in the Secret Pages what you are looking for.

Seek truth over belief

Self-belief is the key to unlocking pure genius!

The greater your self-belief in every area of life, the more infinite the intelligence you can harness from your True Self in that particular area. It is the key that unlocks All Knowing regarding everything.

What holds you back from living your dreams? Fear of failure? Fear of disappointment? Fear to stand alone, to be singled out, rejected by your peers? Those who reject you only do so because they gave up on their dreams and do not want you living yours!

Many things get in the way of allowing self-belief in.

Predominantly, it is your limiting beliefs about yourself that block it from ever entering your space. It is important to be mindful of what seriously blocks self-belief, as follows ...

What Can People Do To Keep Self-Doubt Out?

The secret path to accessing self-belief is contained within the Secret Pages. However, to avoid self-doubt being permanently engaged, consider the following:

1) Your Beliefs Equal Your Reality
Many of our beliefs tell us we are inadequate, no good, and not worthy. Remember, we can easily clear these to make more room for self-belief to enter.

Furthermore, many people feel doomed or cursed, as they never seem to get a break in life. Rather, see your experiences in your life as a reflection of the beliefs you hold. Clearing your beliefs at the Subconscious level will give you access to creating new experiences in your life, ones that reinforce your greatness and therefore your self-belief.

2) Self-Doubt And Beating Yourself Up

Whole Brain Intelligence is a journey of developing and building self-belief. One of the worst things you can do is to constantly doubt yourself, question your every decision, and worst of all to beat yourself up after you make a mistake. These are highly disempowering and the opposite of the name of the game—self-belief.

3) Avoid Comparing Yourself To Other People

hile this has been bred into many of us, comparison creates feelings of self-doubt and inadequacy and is just not necessary. Whether you compare yourself to people who are better or worse, this behavior stems from inadequacy. See yourself as independent of others. Learn to focus inward. It is irrelevant what journey others are on, who they are, what they have, how they look, and so on.

4) Your Thoughts Are Not Who You Are

You have thoughts, but you are not your thoughts. Consider that they belong to your beliefs about yourself rather than your True Self. Stop believing whatever pops into your head and start asking your True Self to uncover: "What is the Truth?"

5) Seeing Others As Experts On Your Life

Yes, other people might be smarter than you, more educated, or even more enlightened, but underneath this exterior you are both the same—you are both an All Knowing True Self, which you are both learning to allow in. Avoid advice on your life, unless it is coming from your own True Self. Trust in your inner voice, as the more you trust it (trust yourself), the stronger it (you) becomes.

6) Science Has Not Yet Mastered Your Reality

Scientific discoveries and academic conclusions are inconclusive until they incorporate the non-physical Universe—thought—into their conclusions. Rely on accessing your All Knowing to determine what does or does not constitute your reality. Scientists still have more to learn.

7) Avoid People Who Attack You

Spend as little time as possible with people who do not recognize your greatness. People who do not see themselves as great have two choices to make themselves feel better:

a) To cut down anyone who shows this up for them; or
b) To learn to see themselves as great.

Unfortunately, most people choose to cut others down rather than working on themselves. Worst of all, this is often done very covertly, without you even noticing. When you feel very drained and weak after spending time with someone, consider that they might not have your best interests at heart. Get present to your interactions with such people and see for yourself how they behave and what effect this has on you. How do they leave you feeling?

8) Scrutinizing Your Genius

Many of your beliefs have you feel that your ideas will

not stand up, that they will be ridiculed by others who know more than you (or think they know more than you). The truth is, genius is within every one of us, and just because someone else has not yet discovered something, or a laboratory has not yet validated what you can see, it does not make your perspectives or inspiration wrong or invalid. Everyone is a genius on the inside; it is time to allow it to speak! And remember, no-one enlightened will ever ridicule you.

How many times do you ask others for their advice? Do you realize the enormous cost this has on your levels of self-belief and your future? If you knew this, you would stop! Rather, seek advice on how best to trust yourself, to access the answers within.

Truth 5

Fields Of Thought

All Knowing is who you are,
Believe in this and you'll go far.
Awake to the truth that all is you,
"Just a figment of the mind" is what's untrue.
Know this, as it will serve you well—
Deep within is an endless well.
It's hard to see the greatness within,
When so many deny themselves a grin.
It's time to grow, let go of the fight,
It's time to shine, to be so bright.
It's your turn now, to tell others what's true—
For when you do, All Knowing is you!
Once you become engaged in Whole Brain
Intelligence, the Universe opens doors for you. This
state of being not only has you bypass your limiting
beliefs about yourself, but it opens you up to a world
without limits.

You are part of pure Consciousness. In this space, all thought is possible—it just arrives.

As a human being, our beliefs filter out different frequencies of intelligence. The clearer our beliefs, the more thought frequencies we get to access.

The truth is, at our core we are not our beliefs—we draw on our belief systems when we believe we have to. When we relate to ourselves as small, we engage our belief systems. It is not a default operating system, but rather a 'broken' way of being.

To bypass your belief system in everyday waking Consciousness, you need to conceive of a reality that is invisible to the naked eye—one that starts in thought, begins to crystallize in your emotions and then is created through your behavior. This is the ultimate manifestation of a human being, where you wield creative forces through your body and into existence.

Begin to see yourself as a creative vessel, unattached to being human. In this space, all thought becomes available, no longer constrained by your filters. See yourself as a vessel for Consciousness rather than a person with a thinking mind. The less you believe has to be true, the freer you are to see yourself as limitless possibility. The less you are attached to, the faster the real truth can be revealed to you.

Physics Or Intention, Is There More?

Physics has been misinterpreted. The laws of nature that people witness are not laws at all, but rather the cause and effect of holding an intention within reality. What people witness is really a product of their knowledge, not physics.

We all want to believe in something and so attachment develops. We need to loosen our grip so a new reality can emerge, one that is malleable. An All Knowing mind sees there is no future and no past—just a light in the moment of here and now. It is in that moment where a genius plants seeds to create new experiences of light.

Your reality is what you believe it to be. The less you believe, the less you conceive. The more you believe, the more of the Universe you can access.

Who said imagination is not real? Your physical reality mirrors what is most commonly believed rather than what is actually possible. Our current understanding of physics is based on only what we are capable of seeing right now—which is based solely on who we believe ourselves to be.

Stay inward-focused, only your journey matters—
no more comparisons!

Why Is It So Important To Remain Unattached To A Fixed Reality?

Every time we assume something to be "right," we limit what is actually possible, constraining our growth and expansion.

We need to make a quantum shift, beginning with dropping "right" and "wrong," "fact" and "fiction," "good" and "bad," and begin working with what works now, remaining open to new ways of understanding.

While we insist that we know what reality consists of, we fool ourselves into being stuck in only that reality. To fool yourself into a fixed reality limits future discoveries, next-level breakthroughs, and ensures your Ego is allowed to dominate your experience of life.

Until we connect to the whole picture, all we can see is a drop in the ocean. If we settle on this drop as reality, we settle for a very small existence.

Keep searching, because there is more, so much more.

The interesting truth, or reality, about physics and the interrelationship with all things is that rather than there being a fixed reality, it is more accurate to say there are colliding versions of reality. What is true for one person is not necessarily true for another.

What becomes available and/or possible is always subject to one's level of awareness, how interconnected one is to the larger picture. The greater one's awareness of their true nature, the more their reality expands.

Reality is in the eyes of the beholder.

Is Physical Reality An Illusion?

What is real? How do we know? Is the physical Universe merely a projection from within the mind? How is this so? What makes this possible? The truth is light. The untruth is the appearance of something other than light, such as the physical Universe. This appearance is created by putting light through a filter called the mind. Just like pushing light through a prism, the mind relays to the conscious awareness—an alternate paradigm to take on reality with depth, texture, and consequence.

There are many 'minds'/perspectives creating many different universes, each with their unique quality of experience.

The truth is that underneath this varied exterior is something invisible and malleable. The physical illusion is perpetuated the more a person holds beliefs about it. The more beliefs we have about our reality, the more real it feels.

Accept others for being on their own journey, as you are on yours

Enlightenment is often accompanied by much laughter, as it is the process of awakening to the unreal nature of the physical Universe, bringing tears of joy in the realization of its true nature, its true nature being 'intelligent awareness.'

Consciousness is the only reality—the rest is 'mind'-made. To know your truth, look beyond what your five senses tell you is real. Look into your imagination, into what is possible—here you will find the truth.

This is the real world, the world made of thought, of pure imagination.

How Do We See With X-ray Vision?

Your mind can literally draw on infinite intelligence, allowing your Consciousness to make the wisest possible decisions. All things are frequencies of information, and as such you can draw on unlimited sources of information from people, places, galaxies and thought forms on any topic and solutions to any problem.

Your Consciousness can engage with the frequency of other people to:

∞ Diagnose the root cause of illness

∞ Remove obstacles to fulfilment and success

∞ Discover who is friend or foe

∞ Perceive Subconscious belief systems

∞ And much, much more

Your Consciousness can engage with the frequency of our planet to:

∞ Discover the truth about our evolution

∞ Solve environmental damage and regenerate nature

∞ Find how best to live harmoniously with all that is natural

> *Pierce the veil of physicality, drawing on these pools of intelligence directly. There you will find all the answers for perfect decisions; everything is information.*

Best of all, your Consciousness can engage with the frequency of Future Outcomes to test the outcomes of your decisions, without causing damage to yourself or your environment in the process. Consciousness is All Knowing!

The plane of All Knowing is a testing ground for new concepts, outcomes of decisions and ideas. As you learn to access your true imagination in the Secret Pages, you can allow your imagination to access this Consciousness, asking to be one with it and use your imagination as a testing ground for what is possible. In a belief-free space, you can see All. Ask in the space of your imagination to highlight the consequences of your decisions, prior to making them. Do not think, it is not intellect we are using now—it is All Knowing, just receive the answers.

Do not allow the greedy to run governments ...
or suffer the consequences

Is There A New Era In Personal Help Coming?

Yes, The All Knowing Mentor!

The True Self of each human being is the architect behind that person's existence. The best way forward in every area of life is known and steered by them (hence intuition). However, of recent years, a large growth in life consultants, coaches, and advisors has surfaced, meeting the increasing needs of our evolution.

Recently, one type of mentoring has stood out more than any other.

This is known as All Knowing Mentoring.

It involves dispensing with expert opinion, theory and hypothesis, and steering a person from the guidance given by their True Self. In a Whole Brain State, when trained sufficiently, the All Knowing Mentor can act as a conduit to another's True Self messages—this is profound.

This style of mentoring consists of one connected All Knowing Mentor acting as the mouthpiece or conduit for another's True Self, to deliver the messages that person is not yet able or willing to perceive for themselves. The only "advice" about a person's life that one should be receiving needs to come directly from their True Self, otherwise it is tainted by the advisor's experiences, limiting beliefs, and stage of evolution.

A new level in life advice has needed to evolve, one unconstrained by past beliefs or concepts of our reality. No-one is better qualified for this role than the True Self of each person. After all, our True Self is All Knowing. The world must become educated in this skill, in all areas of life. Parents, teachers, psychologists, and most of all doctors should be skilled in this ability. It will change the world!

Of course, there is ultimately no substitute for someone being connected themselves, hearing each message for themselves. However, if someone wishes to seek advice outside themselves to aid this transition, let us access advice that is true, getting the words straight from the person's True Self, the 'source's mouth' so to speak.

Welcome to the era of the All Knowing Mentor.

How Is It Possible To Create Perfectly?

A perfect version exists in thought!

There are fields of thought that span the entire breadth of this planet, connecting to others that span even greater distances. They all contain one thing: perfection. Perfection exists in nature everywhere—all around us. It is up to us to move beyond our preconceptions about what is possible and draw on these blueprints of perfection for our life.

Every idea or concept has both sides of the coin—a perfect version of itself and the Ego's version of itself (inadequate, inferior, not suitable). The more a person is in their Ego, the more inferior that person's creations become, accessing the inferior version of an experience or creation.

The less Ego that exists within a person, the closer they are to accessing the perfect version of each creation. All thought already exists.

And so to invent, to create, to mastermind something is to access the perfect version of what is new, being already in existence in these thought fields.

Everything could be as perfect as it is in nature: from our transport, to our food production, our business practices, our health and nutrition, our medical practices, and much more.

Thought Fields—
Frequencies Of
Information

When you see yourself as perfect,
you will access pure perfection.

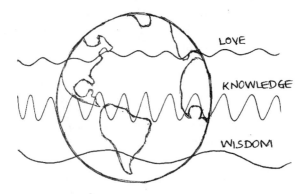

The next revolution in technology will not be electronic; it will be harnessing the power of the human brain to extract and organize Universal Intelligence—All Knowing!

Install beliefs that support you,
rather than continuing to borrow what others believe

173

What Is The Truth About Our Nutrition?

Nutrition is not just about diet, but ultimately about the intake of life. Your health and well-being is weighed against how much of life you are taking in at any given moment. Life is holistic, not reductionist. To live a whole life necessitates being willing and able to take in a whole life. All your senses need sustenance for your whole body to be healthy—it makes sense!

Much emphasis has been placed on a human being's nutrition coming solely from food intake. This is a fallacy. Your nutrition does not just come from what you eat, it is in fact a whole body experience!

Human nutrition is made up of essentially five key elements: Water, Food, Love of Self, Love of the World, and the Sun.

These five key elements match your five physical senses (of course, everything in perfect order!).

Our Five Senses Need Nourishing

∞ Taste = Water for hydration

∞ Smell = Food (fresh, clean produce)

∞ Hear = Self-love (beyond belief to True Self)

∞ See   = Love For Earth (& Others)

∞ Feel   = Sun on your skin

Nutrition through food alone is less important for a
healthy body than the importance of a healthy mind.
Your thoughts are digested too and affect body, mind
and Soul! To restore maximum vitality, and rejuvenate
youth and well-being, you must prioritize the above five
elements into your daily experience.

> ***Self-love is the most important ingredient,
> as it dictates the level of experience in all
> other elements.***

For example, if you experience self-hatred as your
dominant way of being, you will not be attracted toward
good food, good company, or enough water, and you will
experience extremes of either too much sun or
not enough.

Conversely, loving yourself creates a measured dose of
all the intakes—the right amount of sun so as to not
get burned, sufficient hydration (neither too much nor
too little), an attraction toward delicious, wholesome
food, and an appreciation for the world and all that is
available to you.

What Else Do We Need To Know?

There has been much confusion around what it takes to
be healthy: What do I eat? When do I eat it? How much
to eat, and so on. With many of our beliefs driving our

eating decisions, it has been hard to see what actually constitutes being healthy and eating well.

There is a very simple solution—talk to your body!

Consciousness runs throughout our entire body. Everything within and around us is Consciousness. The greater your awareness becomes, the more aspects of Consciousness you can perceive. Your thoughts are just one tiny fragment that exists within Consciousness. Your organs and what they need to survive are also Consciousness—self-aware and therefore able to impart priceless knowledge on exactly what your body needs for sustenance and survival.

When we move into a Whole Brain State, a heightened intuitive awareness, we can bring our awareness to parts of our body to understand how best to thrive. We can elicit information on what to eat, when to eat it, how to prepare and eat it, what our exercise regime should entail—how often and with what intensity. The exact body science is accessible through Whole Brain Intelligence. We are very self-sufficient beings.

Furthermore, the diet you take in serves a fundamental purpose and that is to restore your state of self-belief.

If you eat what makes you unhappy because others say so, we are back to square one—becoming overweight and often lethargic. This is because listening to others over the advice coming from your own body squares you back into self-doubt.

The body tells you what it needs right now. The trouble is not the food itself, but rather your preconceptions about the effect that food will have once eaten. It is not the food that is responsible for weight loss or weight gain, but the reasons why we are eating such foods. We are eating it or avoiding it. The why dictates how your body processes all types of food.

For example, the why behind eating a hamburger might be for the love of the taste. It could also be to revolt against a diet or nutritional pressure from someone in your life, a societal group, or society as a whole. The first why will ensure a smooth processing of this meal.

The second why will ensure all fears of eating such foods are realized. The body gives you the experience you fear or love, just the same as your brain does!

Diet and nutrition come second to the condition or the beliefs held surrounding the types of food consumed. Your metabolism is driven by your perceptions of yourself and how well you believe certain foods can be processed. You can see this all around you—you might put on weight easily just from eating chocolate while your partner stays the same weight no matter how much chocolate they eat. Everybody is different and it is because of the different beliefs and associations we have around different foods that different experiences are created for everyone. Many of our beliefs and associations came from when we were young; and so many are passed down from generation to generation.

Weight loss can easily happen when we alter our belief systems around eating and processing all types of foods.

Eat well—fresh and natural foods—regularly

What Are The Root Causes
Of Eating Disorders?

Celiac Disease—
Root Cause: The belief I am not whole within myself or I believe something is missing from my life.

Dairy Intolerance—
Root Cause: Toxins from breast milk (self-hate), or resentment from not being fed breast milk, which has not yet been removed from the life experience.

Gluten Intolerance—
Root Cause: The belief My self-hate makes me sick to my stomach.

Irritable Bowel Syndrome—
Root Cause: The belief I am not happy/never happy with what I am served in life.

Anorexia—
Root Cause: The belief I am not loveable just as I am.

Are Labels In Our Life Damaging?

Labels restrict reality to what is presumed about that label. Labeling an illness limits how it is healed by how the label is perceived. Labeling a child has them live up to the expectations associated with that label. When you choose a label, you fix a reality, condemning people to what was known at that time about that label, limiting what is really possible for humanity.

Illness

The labels given to illness and disease are at the heart of unwellness, responsible for many people's inability to heal their body. From cancer to multiple sclerosis and so on, these labels carry a death sentence for many.

Naming a disease in such a way makes it more difficult to address the root cause, as many of these names have come to mean 'without cure.'

Instead, it would be far more useful to rename all illnesses and diseases as per the cause behind the symptom. This would give people suffering from these illnesses an idea as to how best to change their perspectives on the illness, and more importantly on their lives, to bring about healing. For Example:

The Flu—My belief system is not my own, it has gripped me.

Tumours—An *I feel stuck and trapped* condition.

Cancer—An *I'm furious at a life event* complex.

Infertility—An *I'm not ready to be a parent* anxiety complex.

The body shows up how you feel; illness is not a death sentence, just a reaction to your thoughts.

Is The Truth About How We Feel Dangerous?

Ignoring how you feel simply perpetuates the experiences you do not want in life. Many of us are unwilling to be honest with ourselves about our true feelings. We pretend the opposite, hoping the truth will go away all by itself. Your body is here to experience. When you deny your body an experience, it gets trapped into your body and therefore into your experience of life.

By looking at the truth, we fear that something terrible may happen, or that we may see the truth about ourselves and dislike it. The truth is, the less you are prepared to look at and address these situations, the more life insists on giving you these experiences so you can heal them. Your True Self does not want a constrained experience of life. Your True Self wants you to be fearless and open to a great life experience.

But this does not come from hiding yourself from past times, denying your true feelings.

Instead, you need to remember:

The truth will set you free!

You will always feel better when you have looked at something you have been hiding from. It is like weight being lifted from your body.

'Looking' takes courage and can also take persistence, as much of the most important work lies buried under several layers. The deeper you go, the cleaner your body becomes. The less emotional blockages you have, the healthier your body becomes and the less you age.

Failure to look at and address these areas causes life experiences which force you to look, sometimes in more extreme conditions. You attract what you believe to be true at the Subconscious level—this is often what you do not want, because you have not healed that part of yourself yet. The less of the past you heal, the more needs that come up for healing.

How Do We Achieve Peace on Earth?

Peace on Earth is a natural extension of inner peace within all of us. It will not be achieved by protests, wishing, being angry, and certainly not by war.

Achieving peace within each one of us is the starting point, and how this is achieved is exactly what this Diary is all about.

We do not experience peace for the simple reason that we feel disconnected. Disconnected from what? We feel disconnected from our origins, from pure Consciousness. Many of us are unaware of this and so we—through our frustrations—try to remedy this feeling by attack, drug abuse, wealth creation, or other self-destructive acts.

Listen to your intuition, it is All Knowing

The truth is, while we feel disconnected from our True Self, we will engage in some form of act to compensate for this disconnection. As this action is coming from "I'm not enough" or a permutation of that, the outcome only brings further disconnection and conflict.

This simplest example of this is when a child feels unloved by a parent. It throws tantrums, refuses to eat, or turns to violence to regain attention.

Adults are no different, except they have far greater power to hurt and destroy those around them. We can all help create peace on Earth by firstly being responsible to find peace within ourselves. No-one will listen to us until we walk the talk first, so lead by example ... "Start with the man in the mirror!" Live a peaceful existence and others will learn to do the same. Each act of violence leads to more acts of violence. Be the leader, not the follower!

Bring peace to others by learning how to help someone else become peaceful within themselves. A connection to one's True Self is the fastest way to achieve this. Learning to work with another person's True Self will fast-track someone's desire to do it for themselves. Bring peace to the world. Help reconnect those who live in disconnection.

Peace is a by-product of Self-Love!
World Peace = Self-Love For All.

Are There Tricks We Should Know About Harnessing The True Self?

Your True Self, your true nature or Soul, can be harnessed in a multitude of ways. How you utilize and draw on your True Self determines the capabilities that become available to you. Housing your True Self on the outside of your body creates a more palpable experience of Universal connection. Housing your True Self throughout your body gives a deeper sense of who you are and what you belong to.

True Self placement gives rise to a whole new frontier of human experience. Ask your True Self of the ideal placement for you in any given moment.

Can Others Harm or Attack Through Their Thoughts?

Harm and damage can come as equally from thoughts and intentions as it can from physical contact. You now know your thoughts can harm you; well, they can also harm others.

Thoughts of hurt, anger and resentment travel across the All Knowing Field, harming the person or people the thoughts are directed toward.

Your beliefs either allow in such attacks, or defend against them.

Be mindful which beliefs you have. The clearer your beliefs are, the more impact your positive thoughts can have on those in need. If you believe in prayer, then it will help the sick or wounded.

If you do not believe your thoughts can heal, then they will not. What you are able to access in this reality is simply a by-product of what your beliefs allow.

Have you ever experienced road rage? Be mindful of what you think, as your thoughts can harm others. Be mindful also of how other people's thoughts are harming you.

What Is The Truth About Enlightenment?

Why do so few people walk the enlightenment path? Don't many religions ask far more of you than simply to love yourself?

There is much misconception around the phenomenon of enlightenment. Many believe it is the time in one's life when you have sacrificed everything that was considered important, when you surrender all your earthly possessions to the needy.

While this may sound enlightened, it is not enlightenment. Enlightenment is a newfound self-awareness. It is where you cease seeing the world as apart from you and begin to recognize the world as you. It is an awareness of your own truth, of who you really are, and an experience of yourself as that.

Some believe enlightenment requires the total denial of happiness and pleasure. Rather, it is the realization that happiness and pleasure come from within. Some believe enlightenment requires sacrifice and compromise. Instead, it is the end of sacrifice and compromise. It is the realization that all that is worthwhile is available to you right now.

> *Enlightenment is a beingness, the greatest beingness one can achieve.*

It requires a belief that deep within you lies greatness.

Within you there lies your True Self, one who is unencumbered by fear, disbelief, self-doubt and self-loathing.

We often view enlightenment as impossible. But the truth is it is inevitable. It is just you who chooses how long it takes. In every moment, you are choosing your path.

> *Each time you choose mediocrity for your life, you slow down your path to enlightenment.*

Every time you allow yourself to doubt, fear, worry or attack, you move further away from your True Self.

> *The pathway to enlightenment is to trust yourself.*

Ask yourself, "How would I live if it were up to me— blocking out other people's versions of reality?"

———————————

Spend time with those who support you

Your True Self, that essence that lies within you, knows the experience of enlightenment. It seeks it, desires it for you all the time. Moments of self-belief, self-knowing, deep love for yourself, your True Self connection, or for that of the natural world around you are moments of enlightenment. We have all had moments such as these at one time or another. But can you imagine a lifetime filled back-to-back with such moments? This is being happy. This is being enlightened!

So what does it mean to know your True Self? Let us explore this in greater depth. Knowing your True Self is connecting with that part of you that is eternal. It can be thought of as a bright white light emanating outward through your entire body—surrounding you. It is pure energy, pure intelligence, pure awareness, and pure Consciousness. It seeks growth by understanding what it means to be a human being. This allows it contrast and relativity to how it currently perceives itself to be.

We are not just our physical bodies—we are more ... much, much more. Our physical body houses this bright white light.

Your True Self experiences life in physical form, giving it perspective and a deep understanding as to its own purpose and role in the ever expanding Universe.

Happiness is its primary objective. Your intuition—the feelings, pictures, or that sense that you perceive from within you—is simply your True Self communicating with you, guiding you always directly to the experience of happiness.

186

No matter what path you have before you, all paths eventually lead to happiness. It is when we fail to listen to our inner voice—our intuition—that suffering becomes the pervasive experience and happiness the exception.

Failing to listen to your intuition—your True Self—is like being Superman all your life, but living as though you are just Clark Kent—is that not the ultimate definition of insanity? It is time to let Superman take center stage and start living as all you can be!

Do not assume you actually know what is in your highest good.

How can you when the bulk of your information is gathered from people in the dark? However, there is a simple test to know for sure if you think you already have all the answers: Are you happy? Always happy?

Your True Self is the driver and the tour guide in your life. You are merely the passenger on the bus!

Many resist the journey toward enlightenment. Many believe that there is too much to give up in order to reach that deeper connection, that Inner Knowing. The joke is you only have to give up those things that make you unhappy!

The greater your connection becomes, the more pro-life you become. All of those self-sabotaging behaviors fade away. Pro-life ways of being will surface, creating fewer negative experiences and making room for constant happiness and fulfilling experiences.

Darkness is a human being stuck, believing
they are alone. Enlightenment is the realization
we are all one and the same. The pathway to
enlightenment is simply recognizing those things
in your life that are real. A life lived with
truth is a life enlightened.

What constitutes 'real' are all those things that your True Self seeks for you. You know what these are; you have experienced them before. You know them by just how great they make you feel: walking through a rainforest, cuddling a puppy, swimming in the ocean, loving your partner, children, and family. There are many experiences on this planet your True Self desires for you, ones far more satisfying than those we sometimes, or often, choose for ourselves.

To seek enlightenment is to seek inner peace, the deepest level of fulfilment, an endless reservoir of happiness and an equilibrium between all those who surround you. To seek enlightenment, is be ALL KNOWING! Isn't that worthwhile!

Dreams – What Are My Dreams About?

Your dreams tell what you've ignored so well,
Your True Self telling you how to be well.
Despite the many themes within a dream,
Or the various symbols you have seen,
The dream is quite unique,
Like the individual that lays asleep.
We don't all share the same beliefs,
Our True Self draws on past defeats.

188

These resemble happenings of the now,
As a sign to say, "Look out now!"
Within these experiences parallels are drawn
To remind us all of who we were born.
These past memories represent
A present to be kept,
Not as a reminder to be wept.
Listen well to be free where you step.
Understanding the true meaning of your dreams
Is not the mystery it may seem.
All you need is your True Self in hand,
Able to decipher the puzzle at hand.
Take pen and paper, a quiet moment for yourself
To reflect on the dream that just took place.
Ask your True Self what it meant,
To avoid any unpleasant experiences in your head.
For all dreams are messages in some way,
To allow life in, or to get out of the way.
Dreams are not the future bedded down,
But rather a signpost of what could be found.
To listen is gold,
To ignore you'll grow old.
But at the end of the day,
You will know you have been told.
It's up to you to hear them clear,
As it's your life you love so dear!

Do not believe what everyone else says about you, or life

Why Violence and 'Evil'?

Why do people hurt other people?

Violence in many forms is a fall-back position when we are out of touch with how we are feeling. Anger at the Self, and feeling weak and humiliated are major causes of violence. It is easier to attack others than to confront who we've been being, how that affects ourselves and those around us. The need or desire to attack another stems from hating a part of ourselves. Rather than feeling OK with all aspects of ourselves, we condemn the other person for showing those parts up for us to see. Our anger is nothing more than a cry for help.

Why is there light and dark, hot and cold?

The origins of the Universe are based in the creation of contrast. This allows experiencing oneself from several standpoints or perspectives. There cannot be a true understanding of our whole nature without contrast.

Black or white are two sides of the same coin.

Why Is 'Evil' Still Playing Out On Earth?

Simply because humanity has not evolved to the point of understanding that violence and aggression is counter-productive, that is not a means to filling the void many of us still carry. Just like a child learning to discover that tantrums do not work, humanity must learn the same thing.

Humanity must learn that our experience in life comes from who we are in life. We experience what we give out to others. Experiencing love and compassion is never created from exchanging violence and aggression.

Where Does 'Evil' Stem From?

Evil stems from self-hate. Self-hate comes from believing we are not enough, not loveable, not worthwhile, and so on. It originates from how those closest to us behaved when we were raised. So it is actually their belief of not enough, not loveable, and not worthwhile that is projected onto us as a child, planting the same seed and thereby passing it down as the next generation's burden.

So what can we do about it?

∞ Raise our children with the awareness that they are pure love.

∞ Teach adults that their beliefs are not real, but simply beliefs—decisions that were made without having any better information at the time. Your beliefs are not you.

∞ Allow enlightened teachers to lead, to be in public view. Many politicians, the media, celebrities, and others are giving people the wrong messages— keeping people trapped in their minds and in a fear-based reality. It is a holding pattern that keeps us all from growing into being more.

∞ Have everyone connect back to their True Self. Teach them how.

What Are Some Of The Decisions That Keep Us Small?

There is one particular concept that has severely damaging consequences on human beings as individuals, families, nations, and our planet as a whole—this is the cost of indecision.

What does this mean?

Before I get deeper, let us draw a parallel here so this concept lands in the way that it must. Imagine a moving car without a driver sitting behind the steering wheel.

Imagine this car is in 'drive' with no driver. Well, liken that to the human race and individuals on a global level as a whole.

Let me explain ...

Your conscious awareness represents a kind of default operating system—akin to leaving a car in drive. But this default setting only knows so much, or very little to put it frankly. It is severely removed from cause and effect, unknowingly heading for disaster, because it knows nothing of its true nature—it is disconnected.

On an individual level, you make countless decisions unknowingly. These decisions take many forms, in particular the ones happening in the background, such as choosing to dismiss feelings in your body, writing them off as nothing; ignoring warning signs in your life experience, pretending it is all nonsense; acting like there is no greater intelligence working within you ...

These are the decisions that do you the most damage, because if they warrant warning, look out, there is trouble.

Let us bring to light what many of these indecisions entail. The classics are:

∞ Experiencing burn-out from trying to create wealth or corporate status.

∞ Taking drugs or alcohol under the delusion that life will still stand as good a chance to be great, that life opportunities will be seen as clearly as before.

∞ Men staring at other women while being in a relationship—seems innocent enough, right? Innocent maybe, but not without its set of consequences.

∞ Ignoring the body's need for rest and relaxation—it can take years off your life.

∞ Sending children to a school solely based on academic excellence as opposed to what environment is most nurturing of their specific needs.

∞ Associating with people who keep putting you down, pretending they know more about life than you.

∞ Over-exercising is often more damaging to well-being than under-exercising.

∞ The most damaging of all indecisions: pretending that our nature is fed by money rather than the natural resources on this planet. We cannot exchange our natural resources for money and expect longevity on this planet.

Spend less time indoors and more time outdoors

It is up to you in every moment to question the long-term consequences of your deliberate decisions, as well as those decisions you are ignoring, pretending they do not even need to be made. Decision and indecision are one and the same—they both create consequences. Become Self-Aware!

A Conversation With The Earth

Help me, help me, hear my call!
We are one, not separate at all.
I am you, you are me,
I urge you to hear my plea.
You are unhappy, that's a fact,
To hurt and punish me will not bring it back.
The truth be known and that's a fact,
Without me, you'll be flat on your back.
Begin to love yourself as the truth,
Not the man you were told you are ...
Nor the woman who sat at the bar.
These people you despise are not who you are,
Rather a memory of someone near or far.
Let in the truth, you are me,
To gladly see how happy we can be!
My shores are fading, my air depleting,
On second coming, you'll be weeping.
The danger ahead shall not be mistaken,

Take time to admire the perfection in nature, it's yours to draw on

If you don't change your ways, you'll be forsaken.
Let it be heard so loud and clear:
I can be here for your future years!
Pay close attention, or you'll be sad,
Make preparations and you'll all be glad.
To mess with me will end in tears,
Imagine a life filled with fears.
This is my final word, so take heed—
Love yourself and I'll stay here!

Look After Nature And It Will Look After You!

How Should We See The Animals On This Planet?

The animals on Earth are our neighbors, not our pets. They belong to Earth, not to humanity.

Many species were here long before humans ever were, and yet humans dominate all species with arrogance, and therefore ignorance. Leave them alone!

The depletion of species on Earth reflects in direct proportion our struggles within. You see, each species has an 'intention,' or an energy, which brings about awareness within us. All animals, every species has a purpose in maintaining balance and harmony as part of the whole ecosystem, more so than our eyes can see.

The Earth: "My species and I are part of an ecology that sustains life for all. It did not happen by accident, nor can we survive by accident. Wake up people—you cannot live without me!"

195

The great elephants are the energy of unity and matriarchal inspiration. When we kill these great ones, we lose that within ourselves.

The sharks in the sea represent the energy and intention behind survival, instincts to eat only what they need and nothing more. And they are being killed off by the millions for non-essential food—ironic!

The great bears of the wilderness, the energy of hibernation—to ponder and rest—the energy of conservation ... they are being depleted.

Our majestic whales, the energy of grace and ease, of uninterrupted flow and harmony, causing no disruption to anyone or anything, are hunted. Can we go with the flow, or do we force ourselves to be on top?

The wise old tigers, an icon for courage, strength and wisdom. How many remain? Again, their population is a match for how these traits exist per capita of human beings, or are actually ceasing to exist at all.

Wake up people, these animals are our friends, our beacons of light, our inner strength. If they die, parts of our experience within dies with them.

The world and everything in it is one
and the same. It is time we realized there
is no distinction between destroying the
earth and destroying ourselves!

What's More Important? Technology Or Wisdom

Technological advancements have long been related to as a measure of society's growth and evolution. Yet there is one thing that surpasses the need for technology, and that is wisdom. Wisdom dictates awareness before one creates a knowing of the consequences of one's actions and creations.

It fosters a greater responsibility to the whole ecosystem, rather than just an individual's ecosystem. Ask yourself, Do I really need this device, this latest gadget? You will be so surprised how little we actually need to survive and enjoy ourselves. It is far more liberating to need less than to hoard more.

What's Missing In Today's Leadership & Government Policies?

There are many in government who lack the ability to recognize the ripple effect of their decisions across space and time—they are unenlightened. So many of the decisions being made lead to the erosion of the well-being of humanity and its environment. This is an urgent call that the politicians of the world be trained in

---

Know you are not but whole unto yourself

All Knowing. They need the clarity and perspective to tick all the boxes, not just the boxes for the here and now.

To have unenlightened leaders is akin to putting your life in the hands of a blind driver.

Seek enlightenment within yourself, become the leader you were chosen to be, steer nations to fulfilment and far greener pastures. Spread the capability of All Knowing to the leaders you know. It is the fastest route to world peace—a world full of enlightened leaders.

The Oxymoron

There are many institutions on Earth fighting for health, well-being and justice who are the very root cause of what they are trying to solve. Many organizations or professions are claiming to be here to clean up the messes they themselves are creating.

Be mindful not to take all things on face value. Use the eyes of intuition to penetrate beyond what is false and see truth. Feel in your heart what is true and work toward that ideal rather than being boxed into systems and institutions that are failing humanity.

If it feels amiss, chances are it is! You have a right to question the status quo.

What's The Fastest Way To Transforming A Nation?

By now it should be obvious that the fastest way to create a new reality is to start removing limiting beliefs in people's minds. So how do you transform a nation into an economic powerhouse, one that is sustainable into the future and environmentally friendly?

That's right, you begin with beliefs!

The new governments of the world will focus their budgets toward helping people overcome their limiting beliefs. After all, it is the beliefs that are reflected into our experiences. It is our beliefs that dictate our behaviors and actions, so why not go straight to the root cause?

Currently, there are governments who prioritize education as a means of improving society, but simply layering education on top of limiting beliefs does not solve poverty, violence, abuse, or greed. Eventually, many of these educated people are overthrown by their limiting beliefs, sabotaging themselves and what is possible, thereby having their education be moot.

But education on top of a supportive, empowering belief system creates economic sustainability for the long term.

Our society reflects what we believe as individuals and what we believe as a society.

Make removing limiting beliefs a part of economic policy; after all, it is at the root cause of exactly how a society functions or does not function. Should it be a government initiative—worldwide?

Why Enlightened Leadership? What Is Different?

To create a healthy society, you need healthy-minded people.

To create healthy-minded people, they need to believe they are healthy. A healthy society creates a healthy economy, because they create no wastage. Only what is needed is created, nothing more, nothing less. A perfect balance of give and take, or should I say "goods and take." A healthy economy supports further healthy decisions.

Healthy decisions come from healthy people who have been taught who they really are. A healthy economy provides funding to teach people what is real. From here, people begin to live on purpose. Living on purpose is a sustainable, ecological way to exist.

Focus on the people and the economy will follow, not the other way around!

What's The Truth About Relationships?

Do not aim to be attractive. True attractiveness comes from within. It is an energetic quality more than a physical attribute. It is the gift your True Self contributes to this world and to those around you. This is the true measure of what is perceived as attractive or not. It is time to unleash your gift. Only a like-minded True Self need recognize it.

Relationships give the ultimate direct experience. We have an innate desire to partner, to mate, and to bond with one another. Why? To procreate? To continue the species?

When you consider what we have covered so far, it seems that there is an even greater reason to partner beyond that of procreation. Consider that the innate drive to procreate is not simply to further the species, but more importantly to continue the access to direct experience.

Without another, your capacity to know who you are and expand is limited to that of your environmental stimulus. You already know we are not a tree, stone, or large body of water, so our environmental reference point is somewhat moot at this point in our evolution.

Using one another as a reference point is far more useful at this phase of our development. We may know we

---

Death is a rebirth of the Soul

are not a rock or stone, but do we know who we are in reference to every aspect of each other?

Who am I compared to the jealousy I see in another?

Who am I relative to the greed in my neighbor? The complexities of human beings give you an almost unlimited access to growth and discovery. Without the continuation of the human race, you face limited True Self development opportunities. The continuation of mankind serves a very simple purpose—growth.

So where now does this leave a 'relationship' between each other?

It might already be clear that everyone in your life is truly a gift, for without them you would not know who you are. Every human being on this planet, whether you have a direct experience with them or not, is ultimately a reference point for you. They are a signpost pointing you in the 'right' direction. The jealous people are highlighting what jealousy brings.

The angry people are showing you what happens when you anger. The generous people are showing you what generosity brings, and so on and so forth.

Without these reference points, you would not truly know who you are in the face of these.

Let us now examine the function or purpose of the intimate relationship and how that can be utilized more powerfully than the current mode of relationship. Intimacy is a level of openness. It is in many ways a measure of our readiness or capacity to surrender and trust in the presence of another human being.

Intimacy is not sex, yet sex can involve intimacy. You need not be 'open' to have sex. This renders it purely a physical exploration rather than a deep emotional and spiritual exercise.

What is love without intimacy? It is nothing more than safety—distant and remote. Intimacy is the next level of friendship; it is where you have made the decision to be real with someone around you.

Love does not require intimacy. Love can be at arm's length. Intimacy is a choice and option of exploration at a much deeper level. It can even be viewed that intimacy is in fact consent to creating a safe space for one another, to mirror each other's deepest aspects and fears. It is like hitting the turbo boost button in any relationship.

Intimacy is the access for you to see aspects of yourself that you have successfully avoided in normal day-to-day life. Call it the magnifying glass of self-discovery.

The aspects of yourself that cause the most problems in your life can often be revealed through intimate situations.

Remember that intimacy does not have to be sexual. Intimacy can be experienced by two platonic friends or colleagues. Could this be why so many of us avoid intimacy? If Subconsciously we all knew how threatened we were in intimate situations, would we not avoid them, sabotage them, and exit them at all costs? Yes, we would and we do!

This is precisely the reason so many sexual relationships fail. One or both parties are prepared to give of themselves only in a physical way. Without the total vulnerability in both parties, sooner or later the other party will no longer be prepared to be the mirror. What does this mean? If both parties are reference points and if only one is reflecting back openness, then there will only be one who can see openness. This is an unsatisfactory situation and will not be tolerated by nature for long periods of time.

The energy in such a dynamic needs to shift and be expressed, not suppressed. The one person "outgrows" the other and moves on to someone who will be a quality mirror back to them.

Can someone learn intimacy? Of course. The question more pertinent to this situation is can they learn in the time period that suits your growth needs? If yes, then you can help transform them into intimate beings. If no, maybe it is time to seek nourishment and growth elsewhere.

What if both parties cannot experience total intimacy?

This can be viewed in two ways:

1) This is a perfect mirror so both parties can see how ineffective each other is being.

2) It is totally dysfunctional, as both parties remain stagnant without the light of openness readiness.

It is time to grow, or grow apart!

Why Have A Relationship?
Acquaintances, Friends And Lovers

It all begins with someone wanting a connection with someone else. A connection is like an echo, an echo of something you believe in. This echo resonates to both parties, assuring them both that they are OK.

A human relationship provides orientation, revealing to each party where they fit—in relationship to one another. The 'sound,' or echo, one party makes to the other is one of agreement and commonality.

During conversation, both parties discover who they are in the face of that situation. For example, one person may be experiencing a career change, while the other is going through a divorce. In this example, the common thread being shown up to both parties in the interaction is why they have been brought together. In this case, showing up why one has felt the need to split up from their job, and why the other split up from their relationship.

This enables one, or sometimes both parties, the chance to recognize in another that which is difficult to see in themselves—the mirror effect. We use this mirror effect all the time to navigate our lives with transparency, and therefore bring awareness to our current state of being.

Alarm bells sound when we meet others who are identical—or in an identical space—to ourselves. This occurrence distorts the blessing—being the experience

---

Telepathy is real—you just need to open your mind to it

of seeing ourselves in another—and often reduces this opportunity to aggression or jealousy instead. Seeing yourself in someone else will always cause a reaction. If you like what you see, you will be driven toward that other person. If you do not like what you see, you will repel almost violently, just like two magnets of equal polarity. We do not like to see the "worst" aspects of ourselves reflected back to us.

The mirror effect guides you along your journey until you discover who you really are. Listening to your inner dialogue when you first meet someone will always highlight which part of you they are reflecting back to you. How often have you criticized someone for not having fashion sense, or for not looking the same way you do? What this reflects to you is simply your struggles with having to look a particular way. Alternatively, you may see someone hurrying or rushing to get somewhere. This will either show up for you whether or not you are pleased with your own pace in life—in particular your pace in that very moment.

Be mindful what you say about others, as it is always—without fail—a reflection, a mirror image of your own need for validation.

It takes allowing yourself to see your own greatness to see it in another. Jealousy, resentment and the like always come from a failure to see yourself in a positive way. The next time you experience any of these emotions, check in with yourself as to where you are frustrated with yourself.

Just noticing the behaviors of others engages the mirror effect. We continuously operate this way until we realize we no longer need other people to lead us back to the truth of who we are.

We are, in truth, everything—for we are part of Consciousness. We are not being everything in every moment, though, and this is where we have the opportunity to take responsibility and choose ways of being that are ecological and support our growth and evolution.

Relationships afford us free advice on how we are moving along our path. Who we have in our lives and how we feel around them are both powerful signposts to discovering which areas of ourselves are in need of evolving and growing.

It is common thought that we only attract like-minded people into our lives. Perhaps one might say we attract those who have an equal amount to discover about themselves as we do.

Romantic relationships are the ultimate mirrors. We learn a lot about ourselves when coupled in such close proximity to another human being—it is permanent mirroring. This allows us the opportunity to get close to the bone of who we are, and who we think we should be. It gives us the time to peel back the layers one at a time until we arrive at the core—where we can create who we wish to be in any moment.

The trouble in a relationship begins when the relationship ceases to reflect the dysfunction and begins perpetuating dysfunction. Allowing yourself to recognize the truth within your relationship is a gift.

Being able to see whether or not a person should be in a relationship with you requires the ability to see yourself as needing nothing and nobody—a True Self space. In this space, clarity exists. There is no room for unnecessary attachment in this space!

Relationships provide insight into who you are in the face of anything. They reveal the truth about how you perceive yourself, who you are in your own mind.

Without this transparency it would be difficult to grow and evolve. Relationships are a useful tool of self-discovery, but only when they are being used for such.

Many people do not understand the true purpose of relationships and abuse them into serving other purposes.

Avoidance is the opposite of self-discovery. Are you in your relationships to avoid yourself, or to see yourself? Are you in relationships with people who reflect your strengths and have you strive higher, or those who put you down and keep you small?

No matter what purpose relationships are fulfilling for you, you will always find yourself eventually.

The answer to a workable relationship is seeing the truth behind the actions of the other party. People disguise their underlying intentions well, especially from themselves. So have yourself be present in every interaction you find yourself involved in. The clues on how compatible you are in this relationship can be found within. If you are feeling unease around this person, it could be time to move on. Trust your feelings.

The clues are always in how you feel. When you feel great around another person, then you are mirroring each other's greatness; when you are constantly feeling weak, helpless or exhausted, you are being taken advantage of. To be taken advantage of means to be used by the other party to avoid having them look at themselves. Another way to describe avoidance is to use a relationship to validate yourself just the way you are, making out the world needs to change before you do.

We can either use relationships to show up exactly where we are at in our growth and evolution, or we can abuse them to hide from who we really are. Of course, the truth can often be unsettling, so we indulge in relationships that have us feel safe in not growing and evolving. These relationships, while providing "comfort," are in fact quite damaging. Any such holding patterns age the body, cause illness, disease and suffering.

Avoidance relationships contain constant abuse of some kind. True relationships, the ones on purpose, are rarely abusive. Abuse is someone desperately hiding from an aspect of themselves. This abuse is dealt out in many forms—physical, verbal, body language, withholding, denying, overpowering, submitting and laying blame ...

Learn to shield yourself from negative thoughts

We are either growing or dying, so ensure your partner is growing as you are!

Is There A Secret To Successful Relationships?

What most do not recognize is that the glue that bonds a relationship together is in fact compatibility between both Souls—the two people's True Selves.

A Soulful Relationship is more about connecting with another whose Soul has evolved equally to yours, a Soul who carries the same purpose in this life experience, rather than satisfying Ego-made checklists.

How can an intimate relationship exist if one Soul wants to experience something opposite from what the other Soul wishes for their being to experience in this lifetime? It cannot!

Finding a comparable Soul, a 'Soul Mate' as some call it, requires truth to be present within you. The times where there is an absence of truth, when your Ego is in charge, you will inevitably attract someone other than your Soul Mate, someone who is a reflection of your inadequacies, rather than a reflection of your true greatness. The trick is to recognize these times and be strong enough to move on.

Continue working on your own evolution, such that you can find a soulful relationship in the future. When you decide that you will not settle for any less, you will be awesomely surprised at how quickly that which you are seeking appears! Your True Self will lead you straight to them.

Soul compatibility means to be with someone who shares an almost identical purpose to that of your own. Discovering who this is requires a deep understanding of yourself—a connection to your own True Self. This requires stillness. Listen to the messages of your body to guide you there. Fears, self-doubt and anxiety will never be present in the place of your Soul connection. Use anxiety and fears to direct you from existing partners toward the one who is most suited to you.

You will feel at ease when you are in the company of your Soul connection. It is a sense of peace, of being home—at one—with each other, your best friend. It is what has you totally at peace with yourself, just as you are. You will experience acceptance of yourself, for they are a mirror image of you. They may not look, dress, work, speak, or act in the way you are accustomed to, but you need to learn to see beyond your past patterns and be open to something more, something better!

Allow yourself the space to discover if who you are with is in truth your perfect match, your Soul Mate.

Remember, if they are not your perfect match, you are not theirs either.

Does Our Relationship Need Protecting?

A relationship is a precious reflection of our True Self.

It must be kept safe at all times. Never allow intruders to disconnect your coupling. There are many out there who have not found this connection for themselves and believe they want yours. Be diligent in protecting the one you love; the circle around you must come first!

Where Has Love Been Hiding?

Love is present everywhere, but mostly under layers of self-hate. We do not see the truth, but rather a version of it—the opposite of the truth. We have been led to believe in our opposite rather than the truth. How did this happen? Dig through the layers to discover self-love!

Which Should Decide? Head Or Heart

Head or heart, head or heart. All relationships come back to which is making the decisions. The purpose of a relationship is companionship for self-exploration, to enjoy a new discovery of what is possible within ourselves. To rule relationships with head over heart is the equivalent of making love with your mind, not your body. To relate to another is to see yourself in them, to be compassionate for their place and love yourself for yours. To judge another is to judge yourself—it is the mirror on the wall that tells all.

We come together for a deeper look, to stand even taller. To cut one another down is to cut yourself down. To allow another to shine allows you to shine. To suppress your emotions, to put on a happy face, breeds distrust, and relationships will fail. To unleash your fears, to confront them all, brings peace and harmony to those who stand tall. Your love for another is rewarded, as those who come next stand even taller. So allow honesty to prevail. So one day soon, only love will prevail.

Is All Attraction Worth Pursuing?

There is much confusion around the interrelationship between men and women; and even same sex relationships. This begins with the misunderstanding of what constitutes attraction versus what represents a purposeful relationship. For most, sparks going off is a telltale sign of attraction or desire for another. Yet these sparks are often sourced from something other than the True Self. Instead, they often result from the mind's vision being met, inadequacies being fulfilled. This attraction, being based on the mind's needs—which are unstable—is dooming the relationship from the very beginning. It is like building a stone bridge in the mud.

Instead, this attraction must be seen through the eyes of intuition—the absence of the intellect—for in this new space one can clearly see the truth of what is real and what is false. Many unfortunate struggles between

---

Karma is the effect you have on the world
with your thoughts and behaviors

213

couples can be avoided by seeing the real person on the inside first, rather than the person on the outside.

What's The Truth About Parenting?

Parenting begins with the knowing that deep within your child is a True Self, a Soul who seeks to experience life through their eyes … and that it chose you as its parents. All children resonate at the heart level with their highest good, meaning that unless steered in a different direction, they instinctively know 'who' they are.

Your job as a parent is to acknowledge the greatness within your child by guiding them to always remembering who they truly are.

A Soul or True Self enters into the physical world at the time of conception. Its journey begins then, not when the baby is born. Some journeys are very short—as in the case of a True Self not making it even to birth.

Some journeys are much longer. As such, the child desires to be recognized as part of the family from that point on. Most people fail to recognize the human being until birth; and even then it is difficult for a child to be seen as great until later in adulthood.

Often a child is not reminded and therefore forgets it has—or is—a True Self, so it can take some reminding for him or her to realize that they are so much larger than the body they see themselves to be. As parents, it is your role to speed up this remembering process as soon as possible, otherwise, the child soon believes all the false beliefs about its abilities and purpose—just like we did. This is when the child takes on many—if not all—of the beliefs the parents live out in their life. And how many parents see themselves as limitless eternal beings?

Not many! Not yet.

The most damaging act a parent can inflict on a child is to have them believe they are in some way not enough.

Some call this being human, and they can be forgiven for believing so, as it is just what they were told as children. But it is not the way it has to stay. We can grow and evolve ourselves, and therefore help our children to grow and evolve far more easily.

How many times do you hear parents say to their children:

∞ "You are not coordinated enough for that!"

∞ "You are just like your father."

∞ "You are much better at maths than art."

∞ "You're not a good speller."

∞ "You can't just have whatever you want.

∞ "Who do you think you are?"

Every time you as a parent label a child in one way or another, you are limiting their beliefs about what is possible for them and their lives. You are effectively sentencing them to a dumbed-down version of life.

***The only one true belief every child should carry
with them on their journey every day, every
month, and every year is this:***

"I am EVERYTHING I choose to be, for the Universe is inside of me."

All other beliefs are limiting in some way or another!

Parenting this way requires you to put your own beliefs aside. Consider that so many of them were made in error, so are in fact false. Do not seek—Consciously or Subconsciously—to validate the life you have lived to date by imposing the very same beliefs you possess onto your children, dooming them to live out their life as you have yours.

How many friends do you have who are in miserable relationships? Look at their parents—how many of them also have miserable relationships? Ask them and you are likely to find a particular belief at the root cause, such as It's better to be miserable than alone. Rather, be amazed at what is possible for your little human beings when you give them a clean palette—with ALL colors still available from which to paint their lives.

It does take courage to allow your child to be great. It takes you knowing that every generation is better off than the last, because so many beliefs held by that generation are corrected by the next.

Concentrate your parenting on being the protector, rather than the teacher. All answers can be felt within your children when they feel safe and supported. Your children need you to be the one who believes in them, so they can all return to being ALL KNOWING Kids!

Your role as the protector is to feed, clothe, and provide shelter for your child, as well as impart essential survival know-how. Do not confuse protecting with convincing your child what is and what is not possible. Allow them to reach new heights and make new discoveries on their own. Do not allow your limited beliefs or understanding to shape and mold what is actually possible in the eyes of your offspring. The sooner they get connected or learn to access their current connection, the sooner they can access all answers within.

A child must be given boundaries, however. These form the basis of their survival teachings. Boundaries create behavioral parameters, and certain behaviors are inappropriate and disharmonious with their environment. All children must learn at a very young age the importance of acting harmoniously with their surrounds.

Children require context with their learning. The why for a child is equally or often more important than the what. How many times do you hear a child asking, "Why can't I have that?" or "Why can't I do that?" Tell them so they know. It may take time or age for them to comprehend and remember—but do not allow yourself to be the judge of when that time is. Offer the why generously.

Children learn by understanding the effect something has—or will have—on them and on what they want.

Your reactions are not your own,
but rather how others have treated you

They either learn by something having a negative effect, or by something having a positive effect. You can teach a child much faster when they can easily understand how they will be affected by acting in a particular way or not; and what they will have or will not have if their behavior persists.

Joy is the most powerful motivator for any child. This is the language and purpose of the True Self, and they are very close to their True Self at this time in their life.

Setting boundaries without crushing a child's belief in themselves requires awareness. Having a child be in fear of you takes away all their power and teaches them one of two things: that they are powerless, or that they need to lash out at authority figures to prove that they are all-powerful. Neither is a desirable outcome for their life.

Fear creates suffering, as it means their life will be led with the intention to avoid that which they fear. Making decisions from this space never leads to fulfilment, because all decisions are to move away from fear and loss, rather than toward peace and happiness.

Empower your child with the realization that they are already powerful, that they already have All Knowing at their disposal if they choose to use it. We all do.

That is the very nature of what it is to be human and in this physical body.

Just because many refuse to acknowledge their own greatness does not mean we are not all great.

The process of remembering who they are, for a child, requires you to allow your child to be among nature as much as possible. Children crave what is 'real' from a very young age. Smothering children with toys is the fastest way to distract them from who they are. Toys are an escape, an avoidance. Over-stimulation from games, electronics and television teaches children that happiness is gained from outside of themselves. Is this not how society lives now, at huge costs? Happiness can be found within. Excitement, a sense of adventure, and stimulation are states of being. Beingness comes from inside, not from around you.

When a child is raised to need things outside themselves, a lifetime dependency is created, a lifetime of neediness. Life's greatest pleasures are sourced from being in love with your surrounding Universe—be that yourself, your friends and family, the natural world we inhabit, and those beautiful life forms that inhabit Earth with us.

I reflect on an example from my wife's childhood—and she is happy for me to tell her story...As a child, she would derive immense pleasure from simply herding the snails in the garden into her little (imaginary) enclosure. She would spend hours "training" them, having conversations with them, and putting them to bed for the next day. No need for TV, toys or computer games ... and imagine her delight each morning when all the snails had "escaped" her (imaginary) enclosure, so she could start all over again!

To remind your child of who and what it is requires massive trust in yourself.

219

You need to trust that deep within you lies an exact blueprint on how to best parent your child. Allow it to bubble up, notice it, and act on it. The more you trust your intuition, the louder and clearer it becomes.

Often your intuition is your child's True Self talking to you instead of your own. Allow this in, nurture it, as it is the secret to Profound Parenting.

It is not uncommon for women during childbirth to access knowledge they never knew they had. Some believe this to be the ancient wisdom of all women who have ever given birth. In real terms, it is the collective Consciousness of giving birth, the very Consciousness that supports and nurtures all women who allow it at such a time.

All parents have it within them to be magical parents. When you can free yourself from how you were raised, or how others say to raise your child, you will find the answers waiting for you. You can feel them as pulses in your body, little signals of information, educating you on how best to parent your child. Go with what feels right!

This is ancient wisdom; it is the very wisdom that created human beings and the very process behind birthing. The more you allow yourself to connect with this energy within, the greater your awareness of it becomes.

Connecting within affords you the exact information you require to grow and nurture your child into everything they are here to be. You will find yourself able to do all kinds of miraculous feats—from knowing the cause of illness or suffering in your child to knowing the most perfect thing to say to ease an upset, to expanding their awareness, and to completely empowering your child to avoid destructive outlets such as bullying, drug abuse, and alcoholism.

Ultimately, you will be able to show them exactly who they really are. It takes two. Learn to access your All Knowing to allow the perfect parent within to emerge.

All parents have it within them to get it right. It is when you ignore the inner whispers—lashing out at how you were raised, or copying verbatim the latest fad parenting technique—that all goes wrong. To be a profound parent requires nothing from anybody else. It just takes you to be in touch with who you really are, the All Knowing within, to recognize how best to show your child who they really are.

It is time you saw your children for who they truly are—enlightened beings and ALL KNOWING!

See yourself as light, as pure Consciousness—ALL is within you

Are Our Children All Knowing?

Every child born plays a vital role in how our future will play out. They will either add to it, be relatively neutral to it (spectators), or they will assist its destruction unconsciously. Which role do you want your child to play?

Most babies are coming into this world unaware of themselves, unaware of their nature and therefore very fragile. There are some babies who remain connected, knowing who they are when in the womb. The decision is yours as parents as to what happens next. To aid your child in remaining connected, it is up to you as parents to see your children as All Knowing beings, but also as beings who still need much reminding as to their true origins.

Remember, your child reflects
back to you who you are being!
Healthy Parents = Healthy Children.

The birthing process is a forgetful one. A child almost loses one hundred percent of their true identity, so it is particularly important to start the remembering process at a young age. Here are some steps parents can take to sow the right seeds for the future:

∞ Reconnect within themselves so it rubs off on the child

∞ Clear their own limiting beliefs so they do not rub off on the child

---

Savor joyful experiences; do not be in a hurry to be elsewhere

- ∞ Learn to clear limiting beliefs that are forming in the Subconscious Mind of their child

- ∞ Train their child to access their own True Self, as described in the Secret Pages

- ∞ Practice stillness so their children can learn to incorporate it into their lives also

Is It Possible To Read Your Child's Mind?

It has been on your wish list for centuries ... From when our babies are first born and you cannot yet differentiate the *I'm hungry* cry from the *I'm tired* cry, or the *Change my nappy, please* cry, or the *I'm in pain* cry. Then there comes the time when we can tell it is the I'm in pain cry but we do not know where the pain is. Wouldn't it be great if pediatricians could read our babies' minds? That would save a lot of tests and processes of elimination, trial and error.

Then there is the boundary pushing, the coping with kindergarten and school, the upsets and accidents, the fights with siblings and friends. If only we knew how best to handle all these.

Then there are the teenage years—I do not even want to start on that one! Imagine if we could read our child's mind to help guide them through that minefield ... Extraordinary!

At this point in our evolution as human beings, through All Knowing, it is actually possible!

So you can, in a Whole Brain State, tune into the thought frequency of your baby to find out what it needs for optimal health during your pregnancy. Or later, when your baby is born, tune in to find out why he or she is crying—do they need food, to be sung to sleep, a nappy change, help during teething? Find out why they are not sleeping through the night.

When your child is upset but not talking to you about their problems, you can tune in to their thought frequency to find out what happened and what will resolve the situation. Tune in to the thought frequency of their True Self to discover how to parent what is in your child's and your highest good.

That is the ultimate in parenting—to be in communication with your child at the True Self level.

It is a whole new relationship, to develop and deepen your connection with your child. This stands you on the most solid of foundations for profound parenting.

Firstly, you can then receive guidance anytime on how to act in your and your child's highest good.

Secondly, your child feels that connection and is able to relax into a deeper relationship with you, as he or she vibrates to a new level of trust between you.

Most importantly, you are now recognizing your child at the very essence of them, seeing them as pure potential —pure possibility. Therefore, you cease to stifle their growth by adding your beliefs into their system. You facilitate their Self Belief, their Whole Brain State and connection with their own True Self throughout their lifetime, giving them access to all the guidance and wisdom they could ever need.

Some babies, when conceived, are one hundred percent connected with their True Self—they see only pure potential and are All Knowing. We can tune into our baby already at this stage—in the womb—using our All Knowing. This helps create a beautiful pregnancy and birth, one without pain and struggle. Then we can facilitate for this connection to remain throughout their lives, rather than allowing societal beliefs to run their generation like they have ours.

Let us allow our children to keep remembering who they truly are—boundless joy, pure love, a True Self experiencing life in a human body. It starts by simply recognizing them as such, communicating with them on that level, allowing them to shine from deep within.

Imagine what a life your child can create for themselves from their pure essence!

How Do We Know How To Parent?

For most parents, parenting comes reactively rather than instinctually. What is the difference? The first is a by-product of our belief systems—societal and individual. The second is connecting with our innate awareness, to parent in a way that supports and nurtures a child's growth and development, a.k.a. intuitive and profound parenting.

Savor your food—eat it slowly

To access your intuition when parenting brings about a completely new awareness. We cease being robots, programmed by our parents' parenting and surrender to the guidance of our child's True Self—their intentions and their greater purpose. A child's True Self—being pure intelligence—wants to work with you in raising their being to either maintain their connection, or reconnect them as soon as the opportunity presents itself. Engaging a child's True Self in the parenting process guarantees the child becomes enlightened, avoiding the self-destructive behaviors that many of us have been stuck with.

Become an All Knowing Parent for your child!

How Do We Affect Our Children?

Your Beingness = Your Child's Behavior

High Level Beingness = High Level Behavior

Low Level Beingness = Low Level Behavior

Health At Home = Health Of Child

Ill At Home = Ill Child

Should I Feel Guilt As A Bad Parent?

A baby's True Self is All Knowing. No surprises can befall it.

Remove the burden of guilt you carry for decisions, bad parenting, abuse, or any other wrongdoing. The True Self forgives you. The person this baby becomes will just need clarity around these issues. To help get them this clarity, talk to their True Self.

Lessons For Education

The human mind is a sponge for information;
But on our own it can lead to dysfunction,
Robbing a life with so much promise—
Learning non-truths has us repeat past patterns,
Creating decisions that make bad things happen.
This old reality doesn't reach the sky,
To live a lie makes decisions that die,
A false reality limits what one knows,
To creating a life that's not in the flow.
The world suffers when truth is not taught,
A message for all—you will have naught.
Scrutinize what you know,
Stop believing just because they told you so.
Opinions are asserted,
Although they should be deserted.
Opinions are not necessary, we all hold the truth,
To become All Knowing is everyone's truth.
It's time to raise the curtain,
So all of us can see for certain.
All the children know more than us all,
To see otherwise will hurt them all.
See them so bright, their glowing light,
To release their burdens in search of what's right.
Get them out of the dark, teach truth from the start,

Tell them the answers come straight from their heart.
Zoom out above and you will plainly see,
There's more to life than a laboratory.
An All Knowing brain can see the light,
It is not deluded by getting it right.
It knows all the answers on the tip of your tongue,
It's time to let the young in and have some fun.
The body can feel the truth from false,
Our intuition keeps us on the pulse.
There is much to be forgotten,
The old patterns that kept us rotten.
See more than you know, and
Allow information to flow.

What Does An ALL KNOWING School Look Like?
A Lesson For The Future ...

What the new school will look like:

∞ Children will be taught to see themselves as more

∞ Self-belief will be taught as the bedrock to all other education

∞ Whole Brain Intelligence will be instrumental to all children

∞ Curriculum will be child-focused, furthering a child toward their Life (Soul) Purpose

∞ The teacher will have expanded belief systems to never close down a child's true capabilities— the All Knowing teacher

- ∞ Schooling will make an evolutionary leap from education to life preparation and enlightenment

- ∞ Every year level will peel away another layer of limiting beliefs

- ∞ The focus will be on accessing knowledge and wisdom for life

- ∞ Education will model experiences, role-playing the crossroads all humans face and how best to navigate such situations—a true training ground for life

- ∞ Children will learn how to see the outcomes of all their decisions to achieve a new level of responsibility to themselves, others, and the environment

Death

Why Do We Lose People We Love?

Every human being faces certain lessons in life. It is the True Self's way of growing to another level. The more lessons learned, the faster the growth and evolution of both the human and the True Self. Intuition is the mouthpiece for the True Self.

It equips the brain with the necessary input, information, wisdom and guidance to ensure the most pertinent lessons are learned, and most hazardous

---

We cause our illness; we can certainly heal it too

mistakes avoided. Intuition is a very natural ability. It is our birthright to have access to the same know-how that our True Self is intrinsically a part of.

However, very few people are raised to nurture and harness their intuition, often ignoring these key messages for the duration of their life. The consequence of denying this information source can be severe. At best, death comes much later in life.

At worst, it takes people in the prime of their life, away from family and loved ones.

So why do we lose the ones we love? Because people are not listening to their True Self's messages! It may be tough to hear, but that is the truth.

It is a True Self's responsibility to keep their body alive as long as possible. The longer the person lives, the more growth can potentially be accomplished.

Sometimes a True Self might choose to "check out early," but this is more the exception than the rule. It can happen for several reasons: drug abuse severing a True Self's connection to the body, a person committing severe crimes, a complete denial of the existence of the True Self.

The majority of deaths occur not because of an absence of the True Self, but rather a denial of True Self. A lack of ability and willingness to allow in the messages—the voice of their True Self—at critical moments.

Our intuition is essential for survival.
The more we listen to it, the longer and
healthier we will live.

Stubbornness and defiance are traits of those ignoring their intuition. These people are often the first to go ...

Disappointment and loss: we often attach
to those things we feel we need for our survival
and happiness. Often, it is these very things that
are the cause of our upsets and disappointments.
Look at what in particular it is about what you
have lost that you believe you are missing within
yourself. You will discover you have it within
to be unleashed.

Is There Life After Death?

Many people fear death because they believe it is going to be painful, depressing, having all their memories flash past them; or because it represents something final, the end, pitch black darkness. The truth of this experience is that it is anything but those things. It certainly does not need to be painful, hurtful or depressing. In fact, it is the opposite—of course, turn it upside down!

Understanding death requires several levels of understanding. The first level is the understanding of the physical illusion. This represents a perspective where human beings become trapped into a mindset that they are physical entities only. This belief perpetrates the next illusion—that for the body to die there must be nothing after that.

Yes, the body dies, but you are not your body—just like you are not your car when it goes. The body dying just ends this particular version of your temporary physical experience. The body has a True Self—you!

The body and True Self are interrelated on many levels. Without understanding this, it is difficult to see the bigger picture of what death actually entails.

The True Self of the body is very light, a bright white light—very powerful, made of pure intelligence. Its density is the opposite of physical matter. In fact, because the True Self is so light, often the body and mind reject it, thinking it is not real, not of the physical dimension. This happens because of the physical illusion. The True Self enters the body just prior to conception and stays locked into the body until just prior to death. The True Self is able to move freely from the body periodically for short periods of time.

Anything longer and the body would not be able to live. The True Self plays multiple roles, many of which are overlooked by human beings, causing immense struggle. The first role is to supply the intelligence necessary to keep the body functioning and growing.

A True Self's energy is a major source of the body's intelligence found within all our cells. The second role is to fuel the heart and mind with intelligence, with information to keep the person growing, prospering, or sometimes just surviving.

Once the body begins to die, the True Self exits in sufficient time. The True Self's awareness from this lifetime, the lessons learned, are carried forward into the next body they inhabit. This is achieved by carrying their resonance into the DNA of the next person, creating an ease of entry, a better start for that lifetime. The DNA is then used by the True Self to fast-track that person's awareness rather than starting completely from scratch every time.

The more lessons we have learned, the more enlightened we have become, and the more advanced we are in our next life experience.

The next level of understanding is how the mind—self-awareness—of a person is reconnected to the True Self, so we can see how life goes on after physical death. The mind—self-awareness as we call it—is lodged temporarily in this Ego for the duration of our lifetime. But it is the True Self's intelligence that powers our brilliance and enlightened wisdom.

This is because the mind's intelligence is limited to this lifetime, whereas a True Self's intelligence is not limited by anything. It is infinite, spanning the far reaches of time and space—pure possibility.

Death is like Sunday. Is Sunday the end of the old week, or the beginning of a new week?

Be patient, there is no hurry

233

Self-awareness close to death allows in True Self intelligence, so we remember (maybe for the first time) who we really are and what we are doing on Earth.

This mind starts anew every time birth happens—like a forgetting machine. This remembering at the time of death separates the mind from the Ego, freeing it back into its original True Self state. From here, the True Self cleanses itself of any debris and experiences the Conscious Mind holds on to, such as fixed perspectives, dreams, desires, and so on.

It seems absurd to spend your entire life acquiring physical possessions when you do not get to take them with you. Why not spend your life acquiring wisdom? It is the only thing we do get to keep!

Death One-on-One ...

I am waking up from the dream that is your life.
I am a new beginning, not the end of life.
I close one reality and open one anew,
The end of a life is not something new.
As your consciousness shifts from one to another,
You open a door that leads to another.
Who is knocking at the door,
It's your True Self who wants to be more!
As you leave this world for the next,
You'll find you remember who you will be next.
You'll be reminded of who you are really,
An All Knowing Universe that sees so clearly.

234

I'm not to be dreaded, not to be feared.
Nor am I to be avoided.
I am a birthright for all living things
To continue growth and discovery with wings.
I am the exit door for those to leave
A life that was spent so painfully.
Exit the stage and you'll be amazed
That it's not the end, just goodbye to the maze.
I can be painful to those who resist life,
But nonchalant to those who love life.
I can become nothing for those who have no fears,
Or pain and anguish for those who carry their years.
Your enlightenment, or absence of,
Dictates all of the above.
Oneness with everything is available right now.
Death is no sideshow, just a taking a bow.
Access All Knowing in the here and now,
And you and I can all be pals.
Some even experience me in a similar state,
Leaving their bodies, existing as space.
Seek to know yourself as more,
Not the beliefs your mind has stored.
You never truly die, it's all a dream,
One your mind so sincerely believes in.
In the end, you are new,
A different version of who you once knew.
Rejoice in the gift of life and you'll be light,
Death and rebirth will feel like flight.
It's time to leave, it's time to go,
All you take with you is what you know!

Business

What's The Shortcut To Achieving Business Success?

Like a human being, a business carries a higher purpose.

This purpose is driven by fulfilling a need, one that this business was created to fulfil. It is this need that defines the purpose of a business.

Similar to the True Self of a human being, the 'higher purpose' guides a business toward the smoothest possible path toward growth and success.

When the owners, managers or shareholders steer a business away from its higher purpose, a business begins to draw on more resources than its environment can sustain. It becomes counter-ecological.

A Universal intention is that all things must operate in harmony with their environment. This ensures everything flourishes, remains sustainable, and is able to receive all the necessary 'environmental' support it requires.

A business' higher purpose is always simple. Knowing the higher purpose of any business creates synergy between business, the population, and the earth.

Earth's resources are dependent on how true everyone is to their own higher purpose. The planet cannot—and will no longer—support people who are in disconnect with its rhythms. Business and government must reconnect to their own highest purpose if balance is to be restored.

A business is guided by its higher purpose. That is its function, its role on Earth. It will not be supported by the collective Consciousness when it travels outside its purpose. Energetic agreement is implicit when something is born into this world.

Synergy between all things occurs when a higher purpose is being executed.

A business supports the growth of its people. However, when a business veers off track, it no longer serves its people. The aim or objective is to have the higher purpose of the business—and that of its people—aligned. It is like having all the legs of a millipede walking in harmony.

When a business acts outside its higher purpose, it no longer acts within its ecosystem—be that staff, finances, production, the natural environment, and so on. This is an epidemic today when you explore the impact modern business is having on everything and everyone.

When a business sells out its higher purpose to pursue the greed of its owners, shareholders, or operators, it has lost its purpose. During this phase, it consumes the energy of all involved to stay alive. This is not the design of the Universe. Where do you see nature acting outside of equilibrium like this?

Look at nature's intelligence, it's yours too

Discovering the higher purpose of a business must be distinguished from the activity of the business. A business' purpose is to satisfy a crucial need within its target audience and its stakeholders. The higher purpose for any business is easily found by asking, "What need does it service?", or better yet "What need was it originally intended to service?" It is the original intention behind the birth of the business.

What purpose does it provide and to whom? Not "What is it doing?", nor "What are its products and services?"

Following the higher purpose equals boom!
Forgetting it, everything goes bust!

Look at so many organizations—even large multinational conglomerates—that have breached their higher purpose in search of fast profits, acting totally inharmoniously with their environment. This has them burn resources—natural, human, and financial—to keep them going.

Ask your All Knowing Self for the perfect blueprint to running your perfect business. See what your business' purpose is!

Businesses acting in balance are far more efficient and profitable. The more ecological and sustainable a business is, the greater its profits.

What Are The Role Of Beliefs In Business?

Limiting beliefs contained within an organization act the same way as limiting beliefs within an individual, deteriorating the productivity of that business as it does over time kill the life of a human being.

A business' success is dependent upon the collective beliefs of all involved. A business, too, is a mirror reflection of its belief system.

An organization, very similar to a person, carries beliefs about itself and what is or is not possible— made up of all the staff, shareholders, and external stakeholders. Self-doubt spread through a business' people, or held by particular business leaders, erodes the possible success of that business. It may believe something consciously, or want to believe something as a group, but it is the true beliefs that make the difference to success or failure.

If many individuals carry the belief that the success of the business is more important than their own well-being, that belief system translates into the business' overall decision-making.

And so, when it comes to making decisions about the environment—its people—the business will always come first. The micro is reflected throughout the macro.

To create the sustainable and ecological growth of any business, you must weed out staff with incongruent belief systems to that of the actual vision and higher purpose of that business. Change the beliefs and you change the reality and future outcomes of that business!

In the near future, recruitment will be based more on what Subconscious beliefs are held by that individual and how malleable they are to changing these key beliefs, and less about what is written on a piece of paper.

Beliefs at the helm that steer businesses wrong:

∞ **Belief:** Money is more important than my health and well-being.
Truth: Money is not your Life Purpose. Without health you won't achieve your Life Purpose. Money is a by-product of being on purpose. Those not on purpose may make money (as many do), but will lose their health in the process.

∞ **Belief:** Competition is something to be feared in this reality.
Truth: Greed will be the undoing in business and life.

∞ **Belief:** I am worth more than my customers.
Truth: A business exists first and foremost to serve customers. This keeps it in balance.

∞ **Belief:** A business is a licence to make profits, no matter what.
Truth: Profit is an insufficient measure of success. Try creating a business that sustains instead of destroys—that's the goal, that's the skill.

∞ **Belief:** I must make this business profitable no matter what it costs.

- ∞ **Truth:** Seek direction from your guidance within, to focus your efforts on a goal that creates balance and equilibrium, rather than one that creates upheaval and stress.

- ∞ **Belief:** My family trust me to do the right thing in business in order to put food on the table.
  Truth: Your family's well-being is a by-product of your well-being. Do not rob them of your life by giving it over to goals that serve no-one's greater purpose.

- ∞ **Belief:** Earth is ours to do with as we please.
  Truth: You were put on Earth, Earth was not put on you. What this means is you are effectively a tenant, renting this space for your self-exploration. Renters' rights do not allow for ownership entitlements.

Can You Read The Energy Or Thought Of A Business In Whole Brain Intelligence?

A business, like a person, is also pure thought. It is the sum energy of all thoughts that belong to it, from its founders to its clients, its staff and more. It is a birth unto itself—separate from its founders like a child is separate from its parents—with its own purpose. It is a pure reflection of all the beliefs held about it! The alignment of its people to its higher purpose, carrying empowering beliefs congruent with its higher purpose,

---

You are Consciousness in many different forms

will create longevity and health. People working to their own agendas will create decay and stagnation.

**_A business is easily understood
when it is perceived as energy._**

The physical world hides the truth in many ways, whereas energy always reveals the truth. When one is capable of seeing the truth in a business, one can easily deduct how to propel it to great heights. A business' 'thought energy' will tell you the perfect version of itself —its production, its hiring, its management, its sales system ... everything!

**_With Whole Brain Intelligence you can quickly
perceive the thought frequencies contained within
a business and identify the fastest route
to sustainable, ecological success._**

This is the new entrepreneur, a mind unlimited by the here and now—The All Knowing Entrepreneur.

The more sensitive one becomes to tuning in to and perceiving thought energy as information, the faster a business can be restored to its intended greatness. The energy of a business is the collective Consciousness of all involved. One can quickly and easily deduce how best to launch a business into enormous success, by accessing or tuning into the collective Consciousness.

Imagine how different Earth—and the global economy—would be if all businesses were being aligned with their highest purpose and were being managed to stay on path!

Can A Business Help Our Community? Are There Tips For The Future?

A wise way forward is to center each business within a community. Through allocation of resources, locally based businesses can contribute income, staff, or other resources toward:

∞ Schools, housing for the homeless, restoring parks, planting more trees, creating farms for produce, re-creating animal habitats (instead of destroying them).

∞ An education series to support new businesses to do the smart thing: "How to be profitable and still environmentally friendly," or "How you can contribute back to the community that supports you." The government can then give tax breaks to businesses participating in such programs. All businesses in the world could be solving many of humanity's dilemmas right now. It takes a smart system to allocate a business to a specific community requirement. This can be government-managed. It is everyone's community, so everyone should be helping. Why leave such important tasks in the hands of one body—your government? Let businesses be involved.

Business 'One-on-One'

"I am intelligence. Look to me for guidance. I will show you a new way, one without struggle, one with precise know-how to deliver on your promise.

"I need to be community-driven—run like a large family business, where my heart is my community. A business run by shareholders has only one primary interest at heart—profit. Profit is the least important factor describing the success of me, the business. Profit does not measure success; it measures how much a customer can be convinced into paying for something above and beyond what it costs the business."

Profit is not an adequate measure of success; rather, a true measure of a business' success is how self-sustaining it is. Is it self-perpetuating? Can it deliver its offering without causing an imbalance to nature, its people, and its customers?

Businesses of today have shut themselves off from what is sustainable. Instead, many pretend that milking the environment to be kept alive is the business' right.

Businesses, like everything, are part of an ecosystem and need to be treated as such. Drivers are given a licence to drive a car based on their ability to drive in an "ecological way" as part of the flow. Should business owners not undertake the same tests and be allocated an equivalent licence? Why are drivers fined hefty amounts for speeding when businesses are getting away with murder? "Every man for himself is a false economy."

What's The Secret To Creating Wealth And Prosperity?

Have you ever pondered why you have major breakthroughs in some areas and none in others? Why does life seem to insist "wrong way, go back" on your plans? Why can determination bring reward in some areas, but not in others? What is at play here and how do you know which direction you should be facing, which path will actually bring the best rewards? Do we really have complete control over our destiny? Which part of us is in control?

Acknowledging the existence of your True Self leads to great things, because it is your True Self who is choosing

---

Money reflects your clarity—become clear to become wealthy

to experience life through your eyes. It is actually your True Self who has the say as to what experience and what desires belong to the bigger picture. Choosing to goal-set or to manifest your desires without consideration from your True Self goes completely against your flow.

How many times have you experienced or heard of others who work themselves to the bone to acquire a new job title, house, or car, only to be struck down with an illness, be left by their spouse, or have the realization that life was much simpler and happier just the way they were. How many people do you know of who have spent all their health accumulating wealth, to only deteriorate to the point of having to spend all their wealth to repair their health.

When disconnected from your True Self, your ambitions and motivations are adopted from others. You inherit them from family, the media, "The Joneses," and Hollywood—all ultimately leading you up the garden path.

True satisfaction—contentment in the purest form—stems from making decisions from a connection with your True Self.

It is the false identity you inherited when you were born that keeps you needing and wanting more.

Your identity by its very nature is inadequate. It knows itself only as what is missing. Your True Self, on the other hand, that part of you that senses its interconnection with everything, is complete—needing nothing else.

246

Manifesting or creating your future experience from a True Self space ensures that what you attract and bring into your life is, firstly, in your Highest Good and, secondly, supported by your True Self—your greatness and your True Self's ability to influence the physical reality surrounding you.

That is not to say that your True Self will not get out of the way for you to create things it does not desire for you. Through dead ends, priceless lessons can be learned, steering you back in the right direction. Many a time you need to discover what you do not want in order to get back on track with what you do want.

It just begs the question: Why manifest the long way—allowing your ambition to create outcomes—when that aspect of you that alters reality, the Universe itself, can support you in accomplishing that which truly FULFILS you?

So let us examine True Self manifesting a little closer.

In simple terms, it is being in complete alignment with what your True Self desires for you at any given moment—your Soul Purpose in other words. It is utilizing what is at your disposal in the here and now.

But it is not doing without. Rather, it is the realization that you already have what you need. In this space, from this space, there is no attachment and therefore pure possibility. Attachment holds us back from seeing all the possibilities surrounding us. Many would be astonished if they knew the goldmine they faced day in and day out.

But attachment to life, looking a particular way, blinds us from living our true purpose and an easy path forward.

Attachment blocks manifesting, stifling your creative prowess. In a clear space, without attachment, fulfilment can exist—because you are present and still. In a space of neediness, life whizzes past you, as you expect that what is around the corner is more gratifying than the now.

Soul manifesting is completion within each moment. Just like being satisfied with every bite you take of your next meal, never needing the meal to be over in order to be content. Achieving this space can only come when you have full trust in your True Self, knowing that your True Self has only your best interests at heart, knowing what you do need and what you do not, what brings you happiness and what does not.

Creating Wealth—Misconceptions

Let us clear up some misconceptions:

∞ I Need Wealth To Be Happy
  This is a false perspective, because money does not affect your belief systems—it just reflects them.

∞ I Need Money To Make A Big Difference On Earth
  Money in the hands of the right people can certainly go to worthwhile causes. Conversely, in the wrong hands it can do the wrong things. The greatest impact you can have on Earth starts with walking the talk. Be the person you believe others should follow. Being this way brings opportunities others do not receive.

∞ I Need Wealth

We constantly emulate what we see in others and make judgments based on that. There are many extremes on Earth—where some have billions, others have millions, and the rest have very little. Find your Life Purpose before you sentence yourself to achieving wealth. You will be surprised to learn how easy it is to enjoy your life when you are on purpose. Here, without attachment, without judgment, and without resistance, wealth can flow naturally. Doing it backwards just hurts endlessly.

Money 'One-On-One'

Wrecked and misunderstood. I was once just a means to an end,
Abused now, holding power over people and nations.
This is not my higher purpose,
I am not to be rationed.
Something needs to change fast.
People struggle so much.
I'm not what you've been told,
The solution to all your woes.
On the contrary, I am not the fix, not the solution ...
Just an insight into your disposition.
How you see yourselves and your worth
Dictates your wallet size and girth.
The solution to your struggles
Is finding clarity within.
I don't bring clarity, it's not something you can buy,

Enlightened Leaders = World Peace

But, when you reach it you and I will fly.
It's difficult to see the positives when I am low,
But this is the best time to find the flow.
If times are tough, get clarity from within,
Find your self-belief if you truly wish to win.
Where don't you believe in yourself?
Where do you believe you must struggle?
I hate to burst your bubble,
It's not necessary that we struggle.
To reverse your financial hole,
Remove the beliefs that see you as small.
See yourself in a new light,
And together we'll shine so bright.

**Seek self-belief in all areas and this clarity will
return you your riches.**

How Do We Hurt
One Another?

Hurting each other comes in infinite forms. Some of
the most damaging ways engaged by the human being
are as follows:

∞ Giving a child a label; limiting who they are in that
   moment to your label (e.g. "You are just like your
   father," or "You're a naughty child," or "You're not that
   bright, are you?")

∞ Telling someone what is or is not possible for them

- ∞ Insisting you know best about another person's Life Purpose

- ∞ Having another feel weak, powerless— or worse—stupid

- ∞ Feeding another human being drugs or alcohol

- ∞ Abusing another by yelling at them, when it is you who has done the wrong thing

- ∞ Not taking responsibility to clean up the messes you make, or the consequences of your actions

- ∞ Abusing positions of authority, having others feel inadequate or at your mercy

The more Stillness you cultivate, the more self-aware you will become, and the more in tune you will be with how you affect your reality. Treat others as you wish to be treated. It is that simple.

How Do We Hurt Ourselves?

There are many things we do in life that have become a way of life, but not healthy for us in any way. Let us explore:

- ∞ Trusting other people over ourselves

- ∞ Believing what others say about us

- ∞ Taking what others say as a fixed reality

- ∞ Trusting our past mistakes to foretell future outcomes

∞ Spending too much time with those who think they are superior to us

∞ Trusting politicians/leaders based on what they say rather than on who they are

∞ Allowing greedy business leaders into positions to make decisions that affect our environment

∞ Staying too long in relationships that bring frustration, sadness, and rarely happiness

∞ Thinking the environment will be here for us no matter what our decisions in life

∞ Treating our children the way we were treated as children

∞ Believing what others experienced to become enlightened must be the only way to become enlightened

∞ Immersing ourselves in other people's dramas to avoid looking at ourselves

∞ Carrying other people's burdens and responsibilities on our shoulders to avoid the confrontation and possible rejection that comes from saying, "Live your own life, so I can live mine."

∞ Following the trends—a sheep mentality. Just because a swarm of people does one thing, does not make it the best thing for you to do

∞ Feeling socially obligated to visit relatives and friends—resentful company is not as good as honest company. Do both a favor and move on

∞ Ignoring your intuition for logic and only what you can see in physical reality

Is There A Fountain Of Youth? How Do We Tap Into It?

What has us stay youthful? Is there a secret to staying young and ageless?

It is all beliefs!

It is believing we need to age that dictates the speed at which we age. It is a commonly held belief that has been passed down from one generation to the other—the more years we have lived, the faster we expect aging to happen.

Ultimately, any beliefs we cling to that are not an accurate reflection of what is true actually age the body in some way.

Self-belief is the one constant that keeps the body's youthful glow, sustaining the body beyond the eighty to one hundred-year mark.

Giving up on yourself, your life, and having no hope or self-love are the greatest sources of aging for the human body.

When healing, address body, mind and Soul
to achieve the best results

Hate and aggression also age the body, but more cause illness than prolong aging.

The secret to remaining youthful is to clear your body of past experiences where you felt hopeless and unloved, as well as to remove any limiting beliefs about who you think you are versus who you really are.

The Soul can only sustain aspects of your physical self when self-belief exists—like the rays of the sun hitting the earth, it is the same. The longer the earth is eclipsed, the less the sun can pour life-giving rays onto our planet. In the same way, the more negative beliefs you carry, the less your Soul can regenerate the cells in your body. Where there is self-doubt, dark patches form in your body. Where there is self-belief, light can rejuvenate your body.

So the secret to anti-aging, or rejuvenating the cells in your body, is to have very clear perspectives about your reality. To see life as painful makes it so. To see it as enjoyable makes it so. To experience hardship can alter the health of your cells when you resist it every step of the way. It is not the hardship that creates aging, but rather our interpretation or perspectives of the hardship that hurts our body.

Clear the years of your past from the cells in your body.

This takes looking back over your life with clear eyes, using True Self to clarify what actually took place rather than what we believed took place at the time.

There is a myth around aging: that we all have to age. Once again, it is someone's ideas and misinterpretation that has created this reality for all who believe it. Throw that one in the trash, right next to: "You can't cure illnesses."

Some common societal beliefs causing unnecessary aging:

∞ **Belief:** It is all downhill after age twenty-five, forty, sixty, etc.
   Truth: Life would be 'up' if you changed this belief!

∞ **Belief:** I must work myself to the bone in order to be successful.
   Truth: Your health must be cherished above all else. For without your health you will not need your wealth

∞ **Belief:** We must put up with things we hate in order to live a life we love.
   Truth: People with this belief tend to live very short lives

∞ **Belief:** This sun is bad for my skin
   Truth: The sun's rays are filled with goodness. For without the sun, life could not exist on Earth. Love its rays, and they will love you!

∞ **Belief:** When I age, I become unattractive.
   Truth: Care less about being attractive and more about becoming wise! Wisdom frees all!

What's The Truth About Sports Performance?

What dictates an athlete's level of performance? How do you go about extending the life of an athlete? How do you break new world records naturally and with ease?

Consider societal belief systems. These are a collective Consciousness held about a thing, an event, or an experience. It is the sum total of what a population believes about a concept; in this case, a sport or level of performance. Being born into a Consciousness often has us get bogged down into believing what others believe. This creates a ceiling, capping our possible reality.

Is it true that new records cannot be broken? Of course not; it happens every year. But is it true that an athlete can shave much more than milliseconds off the world's best time? Yes, of course it is true! While an athlete, pit-crew, coach and, yes, even sports fans believe their reality to be a particular way, it is difficult for an athlete or sports team to do better by more than a mere margin.

Our societal beliefs hold a particular reality in place and we all know how much a supportive or unsupportive crowd at a sports game can affect performance! So it is up to athletes and coaches to prepare their belief systems to become separate and distinct from the collective Consciousness they belong to at the time. As long as they are not buying into other people's reality of what is possible and what has been done in the past, breaking new world records will become commonplace.

The secret to advancing an athlete's career or creating continuous improvement in any sport is to create a new reality between coach and athlete, where they are no longer impacted by societal beliefs (or their own limiting beliefs for that matter!).

All athletes are driven to win. What if athletes could win in their mind first, in that part of the mind that equals our reality? In this case, 'knowing' the win was theirs would instantly make it so in physical reality. It is our reality within that is reflected out there, but only when we are free from Ego ...

Is Suffering Necessary To Grow?

Many people believe life is a challenge, that we are born to suffer; and the more suffering we incur, the more we earn our stripes on Earth ... that suffering is the only prerequisite to growth.

This could not be further from the truth.

Suffering is not a prerequisite to growth, but rather a consequence of resistance to growth. Many civilizations, past and present, grow in leaps and bounds spiritually

---

Let go of "right" and "wrong", it's an illusion

and intellectually, without any suffering at all. This is because they have adapted the basic philosophy that:

> *"I am one with the Universe,*
> *I am in the safe hands of my True Self."*

And so, instead of holding on to physical possessions, their emotional identity, social standing, career opportunities, and so on, they are able to ride the waves—not anchored down by anything.

> *A Soul's journey is to extract a human being from the reality they are being imprisoned into by the Ego. This frees them to then free others and begin creating a new reality, one that brings happiness instead of suffering.*

The journey of being connected to your Soul is not one of sacrifice, but one of gain and fulfilment.

The sacrifice took place years ago, when you chose (mostly Subconsciously) to believe you were someone you are not—not your Soul.

Are We Alone In This Universe?

Our Universe, as discussed, is built upon a field of intelligence, a governing energy system that founded both the physical and non-physical Universe. All physical life, though an illusion in reality, has been imagined by this field as a means to deepen its understanding of itself and its nature. Life as we know it is real, like a dream is real. It is our perceptions of time and space that give physicality its dimension and sense of realism.

Life is born when enough intention and enough thought are determined to be represented as more than Consciousness, as something that can interact with its environment to experience what it means to be in physical existence, filling a void in physical experience.

It is like this: Imagine you have a thought and it is like a bubble leaving your mind. It then collides with a similar bubble of similar intention. This goes on for some time until all the bubbles have fused together creating a weighty entity or thought density. Now we have a thought form, an area of space that represents a belief or concept. As time goes on, this concept evolves as all concepts do, moving toward the next level or phase of existence. From thought to physical reality is a process.

Our Universe, being ancient, has over its years had its fair share of thought forms evolving. To say millions and millions of thought forms have evolved is an understatement. In fact, there is as much life in the Universe as there are 'ideas.' Are we alone?

Nothing is alone in this Universe.

For the whole Universe is predicated upon a birthing intelligence, a cocoon of thought that bursts out new thought, new ideas about itself and new experiences of life. Every 'life form' exists because something existed before it. It is like looking at layers of rock over the many years of Earth's evolution. The top layer of soil exists because of what is underneath that, and so on and so forth. That is how life works.

And life takes on many different forms. Some life represents itself just like a human being, some nothing like us. The nature of evolution dictates the form and also the physical density. Some beings are much closer to Soul energy, therefore less like us in physical appearance or density. The more evolved a species is, the less they require its physical dimension to realize a purpose. The more evolved, the less dense one needs to be.

Many of our neighbors have visited Earth for eons. Some have even played a major role in how the planet has turned out—like having a gardener come and visit once or twice a week. But most of our neighbors are simply curious about how we are evolving. This is because we belong to a Universal ecosystem that has bearings on many other life forms and ecosystems. Just like our local ecosystems affect our countries' or planets' ecosystems, we are all connected in the Universe too.

Many human beings have experienced interactions with our neighbors as a means of evolving much more quickly than those who surround them. There are also those who have simply been in the wrong place at the wrong time. There is much to learn from some of our visiting neighbors, although many are best left out of our thoughts.

How Do I Discover
My Life Purpose?

Many people often wonder: Am I on purpose?

What is my calling and how do I live it? These are
easily some of the most commonly asked questions
by human beings.

But what defines Life Purpose? Is it your career, is it
your accomplishments, or is it your contribution to our
planet or the people around you? The trouble we have
with identifying our Life Purpose is that our mind is
already made up—filled with 'shoulds' and 'should nots.'

Imagine your mind as the windshield, and your
perspectives, opinions, and beliefs are the mud
splattered all over it—stopping you from seeing the
truth of your reality. Well, it is difficult to see clearly if we
are driving a car with a windshield covered in mud!

Living your Life Purpose starts with the removal of your
limiting beliefs about yourself.

Belief systems do not easily allow in the Life Purpose,
for it is something so simple, so perfect, and so beautiful.
Take this as an example: if you have a fixed view that a
career in a multinational company is the greatest goal to
aspire toward, it is then almost impossible to conceive
of a life that is not this. Your ambition could be leading
you up the garden path!

To allow in more information, see yourself as more

Here is a nice story to illustrate the point.

Once upon a time, there was a gray-haired fisherman who would sit by a creek to enjoy catching fish. Then one day, a young, ambitious fellow came across the fisherman and sat down next to him. After a while, the young man said to the fisherman: "You should get a bigger rod." The fisherman replied: "How come?" The young man replied: "To catch a bigger fish."

"Why do I need to catch bigger fish?" asked the fisherman. "So you can sell them at the store!" said the young man. "Why do I want to sell my fish at the store?" asked the fisherman. "So you can make more money!" exclaimed the young man. "Why do I need more money?" asked the fisherman. "That way you can buy a boat!" said the young man.

"Why do I need a boat?" asked the fisherman. "It will allow you to catch more fish to sell at the store," the young man explained. "And why do I need this?" asked the fisherman. "The more fish you catch, the more you sell, the more money you make!" the young man continued. "And why do I need all this?" asked the fisherman.

"So you can retire, of course!" said the young man.

"And why do I want to retire?" asked the fisherman.

"So you can go fishing!" said the young man...

Are YOU going the long way to get what you can have right now?

Your Life Purpose is divine, but it is not defined by a job title or acquisition. Your Soul's objective for your life is never about financial gain, ownership, possession, or any other trigger for attachment.

Your Soul Purpose is grounded in evolution and contribution, in learning lessons to become who you really are. Ironically, living your Life Purpose results in having what you have always wanted anyway—that often means wealth and prosperity.

The vehicle to accomplish these lessons is also not fixed. It may consist of multiple experiences in different countries, over different careers, and many relationships. Life is fluid, ever-changing. We all need to adapt to the changing environment, to the shifting Consciousness that is at our doorstep.

Finding your Life Purpose requires un-attachment to it looking how you think or believe it should look. People waste lifetimes pursuing their so-called dreams in vain, dreams that were compensation to an inadequacy based in their Subconscious belief system. Ambition, greed or jealousy does not lead directly to Life Purpose. They all lead to suffering first.

Steering you toward your Life Purpose is your intuition—the soft whispers from your Soul, your True Self. Their guidance can come in many forms, from experiencing dead ends in life to receiving a flash of genius when you least expect it. All are guidance, steering you in the right direction.

There are very few people walking their Life Purpose right now, which is why human beings live such short lives. Our bodies can only sustain disconnection from our Soul for short periods of time. Aging is disconnection, a distant life force barely able to regenerate the cells of your body and mind.

To assist you to identify your Life Purpose, let go of all the compensations happening in your life. Shine the light of awareness on all your motivations and identify what place they spring from. Any that come from needing approval, respect, admiration, status or validation are leading you up the garden path. It takes courage, but do trust those feelings, those thoughts that relax your body and settle your thinking mind.

These pearls of inspiration are the ones to explore far more closely.

Your purpose is always a simple one, one that brings peace to body, mind, and Soul.

Access All Knowing to put you right on path now.

What Does Our Future Look Like?

Your True Self is working hard to pave a very different future to the one most imminent right now. Currently, humanity, unaware of it, is on a downward spiral, consuming more resources than is sustainable, impregnating new generations with the wrong ideas about life, as well as writing themselves into history as the most self-destructive species the Universe has ever seen.

An enlightened mind is different from any other mind

for one key reason: an enlightened mind can take on knowledge and wisdom unconstrained by a belief system; an unenlightened mind does not. What this means is that your decisions, instead of being more of the same, float in effortlessly, are radically different, fresh and new; and above all are ecological to yourself, others, and the planet.

If your belief system believes money is a priority, then you are limited to survival becoming your future experience. If you believe sex is the fullest expression of the human being, then you cannot allow love for all humanity as the fullest expression of being human.

Our beliefs are our traps right now. Indulge in the smallest possibility that human nature is not flawed, it is just your beliefs that have become flawed and therefore self-destructive. If you know of anyone—be it yourself, your partner, child, or friend—who is a key decision-maker, influencing how society operates, how governments run, how companies utilize resources, and so on, then it is time to take a stand for you to shine your light of awareness onto their path, so that they can see the role they need to play.

The brighter you are, the more they will listen. They will not change as long as their environment accepts the status quo as the only quo. Enlightenment must become the standard mode of operating for a human being, for all human beings.

You can only attract to you that which you believe you are worthy of

Is Our Physical Reality Really Physical?

Are your dreams reality? Are you just waking up when you die? Is this all an elaborate dreamscape?

You are starting to realize that thought is real, that your physical reality is not so real after all. Instead, it is a by-product of the thoughts about it. Reality is a hallucination of the mind, our mind. Your reality resembles what all think it should be and what you believe it is meant to be.

But flesh and death both seem so real. Your reality is thought as you do not know it. It is a complex reality made from powerful intentions. Your reality is created from very advanced thoughts—thoughts that are self-powering, like a dream that has taken on its own momentum, a dream within a dream within a dream.

The Universe has gone from colors seeing themselves as their opposites, to human beings and all other life experiencing itself in essentially an advanced dream sequence. You are not awake, but rather conscious of a dream playing out with you as the centerpiece. In this dream, just like when you do dream, your thoughts create your reality. It is quite sublime!

Who is dreaming this dream?

If your True Self is the dreamer, your life is the dream.

The less you hold on to something being real, the more your imagination creates your reality. The less you continue to interfere, the more this dream actually plays

out just like a dream. It is your beliefs that make this
dream your nightmare. Stop insisting you know best
and you will be showered with gifts, restoring the true
dream once again.

*Become part of this living dream, become
in sync with what your True Self wants to dream.
You will enjoy the rise so much more!*

My Reflections

Why Are So Few Harvesting The 'Fields'?

The Universe is literally infinite frequencies of thought;
infinite number of 'beings' taking many different forms—
from us human beings to the sun at the center of our
Solar System, to the Solar System itself. All are being
governed by Consciousness; Consciousness giving birth
to new thoughts and those thoughts giving birth to new
thoughts, and so on.

What perplexed me was why so few on Earth knew
about this. The answer to my question was: "The human
race suppresses itself, constantly. People, in general,
cannot decide if they are their Ego or their Soul. While
the debate continues, the faculties and abilities that
access the far reaches of the Universe remain unused,
ignored. The 'truth' for many is immensely confronting.
To realize you are infinite and All Knowing is a steep

concept to grasp for those who think they do not even deserve to love themselves."

The Mind Is Untrue

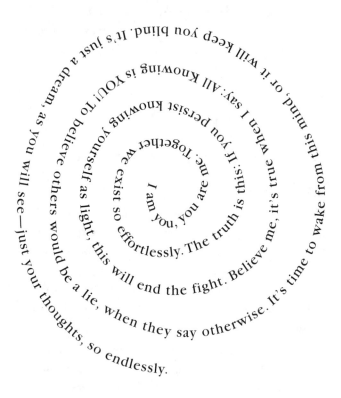

I am you, you are me. Together we exist so effortlessly. The truth is this: If you persist knowing yourself as light, this will end the fight. Believe me, it's true when they say otherwise. It's time to wake from this mind, or it will keep you blind. It's just a dream, as you will see—just your thoughts, so endlessly. All knowing is YOU! To believe others would be a lie, when they say otherwise.

Within the Secret Pages the truth is told ...

Who Am I?

Who Am I?

Who am I? I read the tales of others;
I believe the words they spin.
At the end of the day, I, along with others,
Have thrown my life into the bin.

Who Am I?

I am one with a brother.
An opposite to my other.
Who I am brings pain to the bone,
As what I do, no-one can own.
I am but a question on someone's lips,
A terrible infliction that makes one slip.
Am I Truth? Oh, surely not.
I'm a mirror of what we've all forgot.

Who Am I?

I get you to stare, even though I am bare,
Dominate your world, who else would dare?
On the beach, I lay so bare,
On TV, I'm in my underwear.
One thing's for sure—I'm not how I appear,

You don't need love from others, just love from yourself

I'm certainly not someone you want so near.
Who am I now that ruins one's life?
When all I do is shine my whites.
See past my glowing tan,
As it fools every man ...
For underneath, I am weak,
Always and forever needing another man's cheek.

Who Am I?

He shouts his words into your ear,
One would think you shouldn't be near.
Why hold the one who holds a gun?
When, of what you want, he has none.
It's time to pack; it's time to run,
For he stands there with his jagged gun.
His lips lash at you, to and fro,
Like a whip cracking:"Don't you know?"
Without him
You will grin,
For a new kind of man
You can let in!

Who Am I?

You were told the answer is this,
Yet those you worship can't resist.
From dawn to dusk they will be pissed,
See clearly the you, whom you resist!
Can't you see, your future is bright?
To follow their way will end in fright.

Stand your ground, stand up so tall!
Never need to be one of them at all.

Who Am I?

You are told I'll save your life,
Yet over the years you'll need a wife.
I am told to ease your burdens,
Yet without me, you doubt, you're not certain.
I'm told to bring you happiness,
Yet so many who have me live in sadness.
To let me in just stems from more,
Hear your heart knock at the door.
See me clearly, see me bright,
Allow me to dominate and I'll turn off your light.
I have a purpose, this is true,
But knowing your own will welcome me through.
It's time to change, it's time to view
The immense wisdom inside of you.
Together, me and you will do great things
Without wisdom, we'll become unglued.
Follow your truth, follow your heart,
We'll all be much better, right from the start!

Who Am I?

I know myself to be real, yet the truth is otherwise.
I have an identity; I see it with my eyes.
Beneath my veil lies something else,
It's pure white light, so sure of itself.
"Who am I?" the little voice says,

"I thought I was you, not some endless maze."
Am I just a figment of your mind?
Will I steer you until you are blind?
See past my ways, see beyond the haze,
See the truth of you under this maze.
I don't exist, I am not real,
All I do is play a movie reel.
It's time to say goodbye, it's time to go,
It's time to end the voice that always says "no."

Why Access All Knowing?

Liberation!

All Knowing is the gift of being free from a mind-made jail cell, the end of needing to be someone else, something more, something on top of who you are right here and right now.

Those that live by the guidance that comes from their All Knowing experience far greater purpose in life, a sense of knowing where effort and energy will bring the greatest reward. It is purposeful—no more wasted effort on those things that bring no joy and no reward.

All Knowing provides answers to all your questions.

Infinite intelligence helps you express your purpose with simplicity, grace and ease, accompanied by a feeling of contribution, of moving toward the momentum of your evolution.

All Knowing is the overriding ecology of all that is, a guiding hand so to speak, supervising that all life is getting its fair chance of playing itself out. Life, and the ecosystems that support it, is far too precious to risk being exposed to people who are walking around in the dark.

The brain, on its own, processes information, but it lacks the clarity on its own to project into the future to take life forms and ecosystems into consideration when it creates. The result—destruction!

Only when accessing All Knowing do we find alignment with the collective involved. Only then do we truly know the best possible solution. All Knowing offers solutions to resolve the unease in all facets of life: remedies to cure illness, prevent illness, remove pain and suffering from our experience; answers on how we can get the most from every moment we live. Imagine if stress and anxiety were a thing of the past. Imagine if fear of the unknown was replaced with a sense of calm enthusiasm of what is to come.

All Knowing makes the impossible possible.

Discover outcomes before you make your decisions.

Know well in advance the impact these decisions will have on you now and later. Know the impact also on those around you, the environment, and our ecosystem. Decide on your best course of action without having

---

The mind is not real—see without the mind and you'll see the truth

273

to have experienced the school of hard knocks along the way.

All Knowing provides answers to any question, but not just any answers. It provides answers that are harmonious, ecological. All Knowing does not give solutions that are to the detriment of its surrounding ecology. This intelligence is the source of all creativity, unlimited in its nature.

Do not be afraid of being 'different.'
Different is what is needed right now! The 'same'
has only got us where we are today!

Be able to tune into the reality of other people; become clear as to why they are the way they are. Learn about subjects that no human being is able to impart knowledge on. Decipher the mechanics behind the human body, why it works, where it came from and how you fit into the puzzle.

Understand advanced philosophical realms with ease, as you open yourself up to the truth of who and what you really are.

Shift any negative influences from your life, those that have you feel weak or drained. Learn how best to keep your body healthy, removed from the latest "expert" nutritionist advice. Simplicity ... simplicity all the way!

Discover the secrets behind the science of physical reality, knowing how to create a new reality for yourself. See science as malleable, as building blocks for us all to coordinate at our will.

274

Free yourself from the preset behaviors of your generation. Live in harmony with yourself, separate and independent from how life is "supposed" to be lived. See the truth of your situations, others' intentions, and the real interplay going on around you.

It is OK to move away from what everyone else is doing. What others do is not an indication of what is right, but rather an indication of just what people are willing to accept and allow into their lives. Choose more!

Pierce the veil of perceptions to uncover the truth behind people's words and actions. Energy sees all … total transparency over people, their company's or their nation's intentions and agendas.

See how best to help the medical profession move beyond treating the symptom to treating the root cause of illness.

Tune into the energy of your investments. Get a bird's-eye view of how they are impacted, by what; and when and where to best invest your funds.

Get clear on the difference between inspiration and motivation. Often we are motivated by ideas and concepts that speak to our own needs. Inspiration is a gentle whisper, not a rip-roaring bang. It is subtle, drifting in lightly so as to distinguish it from the thunderous cracks of your brain and Ego (i.e. your identity). Be truly inspired to live out your life in great ways.

Finally, allow in your greatness, so that all areas of your

life can be what your dreams would have them be.

And that is just the beginning!

Do not worry what others think of you, they are just worried you are as lost as they are.

To end all struggle, stop resisting.

Follow your heart and you will start lifting!

Advanced Thought

Can Intuitive Eyes See All?
Energetic Signatures

Everyone is transparent. No-one can hide who they are when you look at them through intuitive eyes, through All Knowing. 'Energetic Signatures' reveal a person's true nature and intentions. No-one can hide behind clever words, a nice suit, or an expensive ad campaign any more. Manipulation can no longer be allowed to exist. Become skilled in seeing Energetic Signatures to see the truth about the people in your life; and especially who you put in power to represent you. The facade must be lifted!

How Can We See Into Our Future?

With Projected Consciousness!

It is just a perception that our perception (sight) is grounded into our physical body. On the contrary, we can shift perspectives (locations of sight and awareness) through our intention and belief system.

Some call this Remote Viewing. It is like accessing wireless cameras anywhere in the world or space. We can use our True Self to position our perspectives anywhere we want. The All Knowing field makes this possible. You must first believe you are more than your physical body for this to be possible.

The present moment dictates all future moments – choose wisely who you are and what you do in this moment

Letting Go Of Time Altogether

We currently experience ourselves on a timeline—what was in the past, what is right now and will be in the future. This is actually a belief system. Time is a way of compartmentalizing what the mind perceives in front of it—box it, label it and it is sorted. This is a very inefficient way to exist. Instead, try to imagine seeing all of time, but focusing on the right now.

What this means is no longer categorizing events into time slots, but rather surveying the field of time as one spectrum—a composite of events—not linear, but immediate. This allows you to see all possibility in a moment, choosing which to experience in the now. It does take practice, but can easily be done after some training.

Can We Change Our Future? Re-Plotting Your Path

Design your own life!

It is time for us all to play a vital role in the consequences of our decision-making. It is time we access a very real aspect of our Consciousness—time.

Every decision, large or small, plays a vital role in dictating how we then experience consequences. There are those decisions that create pleasing consequences, and there are other decisions—the ones most commonly being made at this time—that lead to frightful consequences.

Knowing which decision leads to which outcome no longer needs to be a mystery. Life is not about playing Russian roulette with your decisions. Every human being has the capability to move beyond their own thoughts, their own present reality, to witness the consequences of their decisions in the now. Make it part of your life skills and consider it a prerequisite for leadership roles.

Practicing this ability hones it to a fine art. After all, it is exactly where your intuition comes from. But now it is time to play an active role in that intuitive process.

All Knowing grants you the capability to see what the outcome can be, depending on which decision is made in the present.

The applications of projection are limitless, as are the possibilities.

Access the future in the now;
learn to compress time.

In All Knowing, past, present, and future exist as one.

Therefore, the outcomes of all your future decisions can be seen in this space. Not only can you replot your life based on how different decisions create different futures, you can learn to access teachings you will not normally get until the future, in the here and now. This not only helps to compress time in your reality, but it also saves you and others lots of trial and error—and heartache.

Bring lessons back from the future.
Become a time traveler!

Can We See Our Child's Future And Change It?

The skills discussed so far give parents a most profound advantage in parenting their children. We have discussed the ability to re-plot your own life through seeing the future; now consider being there for your children by helping them re-plot theirs.

Consider your ability has you avoid unnecessary potholes.

Well, you can help your child avoid moving in a direction that leads to hardship or deterioration for themselves and those around them. You can help plot a path that avoids disempowering ambition; drug or alcohol abuse; being in "the wrong place at the wrong time" ... and the list goes on.

N.B.: This process can become collaborative at different ages and can be independently done by children from eight to ten years of age.

To see yourself as more allows more in. To see your children as more expands their horizons, to live a life beyond your beliefs and ambitions.

Can I Teach Straight From ALL KNOWING?

As men and women become more and more practiced at accessing their All Knowing, a new era in teachers will arise—the True Self teacher.

This is where the Conscious Mind learns to accept itself as its higher aspect, or All Knowing Self. This pure aspect uses the human mouth to speak directly to its audience. You have seen this with enlightened masters, but what

---

Fate is listening to your True Self right now

about in schools and universities? Isn't it upon us to be enlightened in all areas of education?

Is There A Rhythm To Life?

They are called Flows!

Our survival throughout history has been reliant upon knowing ourselves, our situation, our landscape, threats, and opportunities. But a new level of awareness beckons us all. Rather than pre-empting our every next move, we can awaken a state of being that moves with the energy flows of our world. There are currents and flows that exist within ourselves and around us, connecting us all.

These currents can be described as ways forward with grace and ease.

These do not take away free will,
but rather offer an alternative to free will.

This alternative is supported by the Universe, the coincidences and synchronicities that you might be used to experiencing—like a divine matrix, organizing life for a greater purpose. It is what works.

The guiding principle behind this mechanism is allowing all intentions—and therefore Soul Purpose—to come to fruition. Free will, on the other hand, can destroy harmony and balance. Free will can be used as a buzz-word for ignorance. Harmony and flow is enlightenment. Your resistance to this is the need to be in control, in the driver's seat. This is a very old way of being, which accounts for the lack we experience in our lives. Control is a contradiction to abundance.

A group belief, current in humanity, particularly in Western cultures, is: "I must control my life to enjoy it to the fullest." This is flawed, because it does not take into account the coinciding influences occurring in and around you. We are not alone; we are all playing out life together.

Think of what would happen to everyone getting to work on time if the public transport system insisted on free will!

We all can learn to be sensitive to these flows, if we all learn to surrender our desire for absolute control over our lives.

The Secret Pages

Private & Confidential

Contained herein are the secret
steps to accessing ALL KNOWING.

There are three secrets just for you;

Secret truths to unlock the real you.

Practice these secrets each day,

Believe in yourself in every way.

Watch soon, as you exit
your cocoon.

An All Knowing being you are,

Someone destined to go far!

Remember, When Accessing All Knowing:

∞ Be PATIENT with yourself—like a child learning to walk for the first time

∞ Be ALLOWING of information to flow—as with falling asleep, "trying" is counterproductive

∞ Be KIND to yourself—self belief-strengthens your connection, self-doubt weakens it

∞ Be TRUE to yourself—give yourself the time and space you deserve for this training

Secret 1: Accessing Pure Consciousness

Ego Removal

You are about to access an energy system that we all belong to, but very few of us have been able to draw on in our daily lives. This book has aided this process dramatically. This energy frequency is pure Consciousness—the energy of All Knowing itself.

It is used to create an Ego-free space. It is pure light, a cleansing energy designed to bring light where there is Darkness.

Knowledge is everywhere there is energy, Earth in one giant library

285

There are several key applications, as follows:

∞ It creates an instantly still mind, a space to access All Knowing.

∞ It takes negative thought energy out of your body, allowing faster healing.

∞ It turns dark thoughts into positive thoughts.

∞ It is great for helping animals heal and live healthier lives.

Best of all it helps remove the Ego from interfering with your connection to your True Self.

Exercise:

In this exercise we will use Pure Consciousness to cleanse your body of the Ego.

Begin with the specific intention;

For example: "Take my self-doubt away from my thoughts, removing my Ego as well."

The sharper your intention when using this energy, the better the outcome.

Put your hands up in front of you, approximately six to eight inches apart, as seen above.

Ask in your thoughts and intentions:

> ***"Please bring pure Consciousness
> between my hands."***

Repeat this until you feel the energy build. It may feel warm and tingly, like two opposing magnets in your hands. This energy is Consciousness itself, the nonphysical Universe you are intrinsically a part of.

Note: you may feel it in a variety of other ways, or you may not perceive anything at all at first. Your sensitivity to this will increase the more you practice.

To clear your Ego away from your body:

∞ Bring your hands containing the ball of pure Consciousness over your head, holding the intention that all negative energy and your Ego are absorbed into the pure Consciousness energy. You may sense this process happening. It is powerful to place your awareness here to perceive what is transpiring.

∞ Once you feel the negativity is absorbed, raise your hands back over your head, intending to cleanse all this energy back into the Universal Field of pure Consciousness above your head, like a cloud hovering above (or straight into the sun).

The Ego Energy

∞ Repeat this process over your stomach area, then your chest and heart area as well, bringing in a new ball of energy prior to moving from one body part to the next.

This energy is powerful, so try it on your children and pets too—do not leave them out!

Use this process to restore a calm and centered space before getting answers from within, and especially any time you feel that surge of anger or emotion.

Secret 2: Accessing Self-Belief

The good news is that, despite layer upon layer of limiting beliefs that many of us still carry with us, or the lifetime of self-doubt many of us have experienced, self-belief is readily available to us all.

How?

Remember, you are the personification of the entire Universe—meaning, what exists within the Universe also exists within you. As self-belief is a concept that already exists within the Universe, it too exists within you. It is an energy frequency that exists within and all around us. It gives us the access to Whole Brain Intelligence, a springboard to unlimited imagination, access to the truth within.

So how do you harness what lies within?

It is quite straightforward.

Similar to your Ego-removal exercise, where you accessed pure, All Knowing Consciousness, you will once again place both hands in front of you, ready to bring in the thought frequency of Self-Belief. Once your

---

We are all thought creations—we think, so we are ...
choose your thoughts carefully

hands are in front of you, as per the diagram, hold the intention for your True Self to support this exercise, requesting that they bring the energy of Self-Belief between your hands.

Ask: "Please bring the energy of Self-Belief between my hands." Repeat this request three to four times, until you feel the presence of the energy.

Once you feel this energy present, simply raise your hands and bring it over your head. Hold your hands in this position as long as you like, until you feel that subtle stillness and precision within the mind.

It generally takes between five to fifteen seconds for this to activate your Whole Brain State. From this space anything becomes possible.

Secret 3: Accessing All Knowing, The True Self!

Here you will learn how to access the ALL KNOWING within.

You may wish to read through the whole exercise prior to doing it, as well as having pen and paper at the ready. This exercise requires drawing on the previous exercise.

Once again, you will bring pure Consciousness between your hands and raise it around your head.

But this time your intention is not to remove Ego, but to connect to your True Self for answers!

Exercise – Part 1

∞ Bring Pure Consciousness between your hands.

∞ Bring your hands and this energy over and around your head.

∞ Then say:
   "I now experience myself as All Knowing Pure Consciousness."

∞ Repeat this as needed until you feel the space shift.

You are now about to engage your Whole Brain
Intelligence by connecting to All Knowing, your True Self.

Exercise – Part 2

Following on from the previous exercise, having
said "I now experience myself as All Knowing, pure
Consciousness," you can now begin to solidify your
connection back to your True Self.

Your True Self is the All Knowing aspect of you. In this
space, you, together with your True Self, can answer any
question you could possibly conceive of. So draw on
your True Self often!

Once in this new space of clarity, ask:

"Please, may I connect with my True Self?" or simply
hold an intention to be connected to your True Self
through this space; either one will work.

To begin, simply be with this space, allowing it to be as
it is—No expectations and no trying!

You may wish to write down your experiences, jotting
down any images, colors, or messages you experience.

When you feel ready, begin asking your True Self any
question that comes to mind. A great question to start
with is "What question should I ask now?" See what
messages or information your True Self has for you
right now.

If all you have experienced is a soft, calming energy, then keep going—you are on the right track.

Sometimes our fears or beliefs halt this process, so remember to keep clearing your Ego. We recommend to keep practicing, as it can take the time where you are just about to give up, where you have let go of all expectations, for this process to work in its entirety. The less pressure you place on this process, the faster you will connect to All Knowing.

Below I have prepared an example of questions you may wish to use in the routine of asking your True Self every day:

∞ What messages do I need to know about my day today?

∞ How do I make the most of my day?

∞ How do I be my True Self today?

Alternatively, ask them directly, "What question should I be asking every day?"

Congratulations!

It is time to become self-sufficient, exploring what is your truth!

This process is a true gift. It will help create miracles in your life. Follow your True Self's guidance and you will always be profoundly better off! You will be guided toward the richest path to happiness and fulfilment.

Enjoy your liberation! Explore to your heart's content!

Giving = Receiving ... they are one and the same

For additional support with these exercises, come and visit: www.AllKnowingDiary.com

Conclusions

What Is The Upside Of Walking Your Own Path?

Many people are afraid to let in something as advanced as All Knowing—not because it is not real, but because it is *too* real. It is threatening and confronting to the status quo. Our inability to let in radically advanced concepts stems from our beliefs around having to conform to be accepted. It is a commonly held belief that "Without the support of others, I am a nobody." Yet this is completely untrue.

If it were not for the visionaries throughout history straying from the flock, some of our greatest insights, inventions, and know-how would remain unknown and unavailable. To this day, our lives would be empty because of it.

To be a visionary is great, to pave the way for others is desirable—inspirational. To invent new ways of looking at life is what is needed right now. One cannot solve today's problems with the same thinking that created them. Instead, we need revolutionary thinkers.

We need to change our entire belief system around, so rather than questioning everything a visionary says, we embrace them instead—innocent until proven unnecessary. Give all the visionaries a chance to shine; do not take this away from them.

We condemn what is new too quickly, and everyone suffers because of it. Take a glance at the material here. It is revolutionary, it is new in its nature, almost foreign in some ways. Is that not what is needed to make new decisions, to create new behaviors that generate different outcomes? It is precisely what is needed!

Let us pioneers do what we do best, to allow you to do what you do best. You, as the next wave of pioneers, can pass this on to the people who look to you for answers.

Good luck!

Next Steps

The information contained in this All Knowing Diary was discovered by a connection from the author to his Soul or True Self. It is something that is available to all human beings, something we have nearly all forgotten how to do.

Just imagine what difference it would make to your life, your family, your world, if you could do the same—to have unlimited information at your fingertips!

Everything would change; nothing would remain the same.

The Secret Pages in this book will have you triumph in re-establishing this connection for yourself. The steps shown are the very same used to bring this book to light. To ignore them, to dismiss them, would be tragic.

It would be to write-off a new future for us all, one so much brighter than the one currently on its way.

To utilize these tools, to harvest their wealth, everything and anything becomes possible! I sincerely encourage everyone to re-read this book, as there is much to absorb from just one read. Practice diligently the exercises contained, and miracles will begin to happen in your daily life.

Infinite possibilities literally exist all around you. It is up to you to reach up and bring them through the antenna we call our 'Brain.'

We all have immeasurable capabilities. We have what our True Self has; after all, we are our True Self. But while we relate to ourselves as 'only human,' we sentence ourselves and others to a life of mediocrity.

The information contained within this book can set you free—free to expand your life experience and free to live what represents a dream opportunity on Earth.

It does take courage to realize "What if this is a better way? Perhaps my way isn't all there is?", as we often fear disappointment. But then again, we are already experiencing disappointment in our lives as it is. In realizing there could be more than we currently know, we create a space where we can be shown how miracles actually happen and how fast they can happen when you and your True Self are being one. You have experienced struggle, now it is time to experience life anew.

If you take the same intelligence that created this world we live in and add a drop or two into your decision-making, you cannot help but make life better!

Please help spread the word to many others about this Diary. Purchase a copy for friends, family and even work colleagues—it makes a great gift. The messages are for everyone: young, old, skeptical, receptive, or anyone in between.

There is no greater gift to give than a gift of All Knowing.

"Give a word of wisdom and they'll know where to turn ... teach them how to access wisdom and they'll never turn back!"

It is our ongoing commitment to you to help everyone realize and experience their True Self Purpose. We are here to help people all over the planet live a life connected to their higher intelligence wherever possible, and so we have built a support program to make this ambition achievable.

You may want further All Knowing Training, a one-on-one session with an All Knowing Mentor, to be part of group workshops to meet others who are on this journey—other like-minded Souls. Or, for those who love this work, you may wish to become an All Knowing Mentor—there is much to explore. The adventure just gets better from here!

I thank you for joining me on this most incredible adventure. Let it be the ride of your life, as it has certainly been mine.

Let us help support you in fulfilling your Life Purpose.

There is a whole new adventure waiting for you at:

www.AllKnowingDiary.com

Until we meet again, with much love and gratitude,

Daniel Rechnitzer

The All Knowing Diary

Become ALL KNOWING Courses

Make The All Knowing Diary A Reality In Your Everyday Life!

The skills and abilities presented here are real; they are not fiction or fantasy. What they represent are our innate capabilities. Unfortunately, after so many years of false beliefs being allowed to surface, many of these abilities lie hidden and dormant—buried within.

All Knowing—to have all the right answers to enable the best possible decisions—is yours to access. To cure illness within yourself is also yours to access. To know in advance of time the outcomes your decisions will bring into life is yours to access. To see in the present all possibilities surrounding you financially, in your relationships, and in your health is also yours to access. To become an All Knowing being—one capable of moving beyond time and space—avoiding mistakes and mishaps, and living your life fully on purpose in each moment is yours to access.

Seeing yourself as more in each moment creates a richer experience of life. Stripping yourself of your limiting beliefs, past patterns, and the behaviors and perspectives that cloud the true you is easily attainable.

No more questioning yourself, no more second-guessing yourself—knowing in every moment the best decision to make, the best thing to say, the best way forward, one that carves a new future—is yours to be experienced. There is no longer ever a need to go without, to be without answers, to be without understanding—it's all at your fingertips now.

Return to your True Self—one of infinite possibilities, pure insight, wisdom and truth. This is you, the real you, and it's yours to access now!

On our website you will find everything you need to support you in achieving and maintaining your connection to All Knowing and your Soul Purpose.

Get access to:

∞ Question and answer forums

∞ An All Knowing Mentor to get you on the path to discovering your Soul Purpose

∞ Insightful articles and videos

∞ The Advanced Training programs on offer

∞ All Knowing For Kids courses

∞ Participate in teleconferences with the author and fellow book fans

And many more ...

Be supported on your journey ahead!

All Knowing transforms people from who they currently believe themselves to be into sublime All Knowing beings—capable of extraordinary talents, able to live their life on purpose, seeing themselves as their True Selves. From learning how to 'tune in' to new frequencies of information, to applying All Knowing to your business and finances, to becoming an All Knowing Mentor capable of steering others through the wisdom and guidance of their own True Self—you'll find it all online at: www.AllKnowingDiary.com

See Also:

Natural
Pain Free
Birth
...A Soul's Journey To Earth

Discover The Miracle Of A Soul
Conversation With Your Baby
By Sonja & Oliver Rechnitzer

Purchase your copy at all major book stores or visit:
www.NaturalPainFreeBirth.com